MODERN T

*To Jania—
Love and light
on your new
journey!*

"...BECAUSE YOU CAN!"

Ulrike

U L R I K E

Copyright © 2012 Ulrike
All rights reserved.

ISBN: 1466345918
ISBN-13: 9781466345911
LCCN: 2011917397
CreateSpace, North Charleston, SC

CONTENTS

Foreword v

Introduction vii

Chapter 1 1
Mental House Cleaning

Chapter 2 19
Beliefs

Chapter 3 39
Happiness

Chapter 4 55
Desire, Imagination, and Visualization

Chapter 5 75
You Are Important

Chapter 6 97
Thought and its Correct Application

Chapter 7 117
Fear and Doubt

Chapter 8 135
Appreciation and Gratitude

Chapter 9 . . . . **153**
Mental Work

Chapter 10 . . . . **171**
Abundance

Chapter 11 . . . . **191**
Relationships

Chapter 12 . . . .**217**
The True Meaning of Love

Chapter 13 . . . .**231**
Well-Being

Chapter 14 . . . .**259**
The Universe

Chapter 15 . . . .**277**
The Laws of the Universe

Chapter 16 . . . .**303**
Consciousness

Chapter 17 . . . .**319**
Sense

Chapter 18 . . . .**337**
Your World, Inside and Out

Chapter 19 . . . .**353**
The Spider Effect

FOREWORD

> "All life is an experiment. The more experiments you make the better."
> *—Ralph Waldo Emerson*

As I review the chapters before I send them off to the publisher, I realize that I didn't write this book for any specific person, nor was I inspired by a certain event.

I wrote this book because everything I have studied, learned, and applied over the years was pent up in my mind. All of the knowledge and daily practice of these facts have helped me to better myself and my surroundings—my whole life.

It has drastically altered my perception of the Universe.

This knowing was stored and categorized in my subconscious, and I had to let it out creatively. Everything pressed in me for expression.

I needed to share what I have learned, proved to be true, and enjoyed. And in the process I knew that even if only one person reaps the benefits, my work would be done.

The thoughts I have put on paper are for you. They are my thoughts made usable for everyone who is searching. So here are my questions to you:

Do you examine your thoughts? Would you like to know who and what you are? Do you want to find your true purpose?

If the answer is yes, you came to the right place. We shall begin this journey together!

Namaste**

> "Look deep into nature, and then you will understand everything better."
> *—Albert Einstein*

INTRODUCTION

All of us have accumulated a lifetime of mental impressions, beliefs, and opinions, but we have not always been diligent in discriminating between right thinking and wrong thinking. We have been negligent in choosing the right attitude, thoughts, and paths, and we have been avoiding painful issues. The list goes on and on.

So it stands to reason that all self-improvement has to start with a rigorous **MENTAL HOUSE CLEANING.**

We have to take a sincere look at the **BELIEFS** that we have to empty out because we are in the pursuit of **HAPPINESS.** It is our goal in life.

We all have **DESIRES** and we can accomplish them. However, we have to know the process of achieving these desires.

The journey to betterment starts with the realization that **YOU ARE IMPORTANT** and the knowledge of the strength that **THE POWER OF YOUR THOUGHT** has when used correctly.

The problem is that **FEAR AND DOUBT** gets in our way, and we do not have enough **APPRECIATION AND GRATITUDE** for all the good we receive on a daily basis. So we engage in **MENTAL WORK** in order to achieve **ABUNDANCE,** an abundant life that includes everything, not just material riches.

"...because you can!"

We certainly are in agreement that we have to work on our **RELATIONSHIPS** not only with others, but also with ourselves. We have to realize that **THE TRUE MEANING OF LOVE** is more than infatuation. In its truest sense, Love is the mother of all creation.

As we move along in this journey and establish a higher sense of our ability to cause (i.e., causing everything that we experience), we want to make sure we understand what role our thoughts play in our overall **WELL-BEING.** This, of course, includes our health, vigor, strength, and general wellness.

Now that we have worked on the so-called worldly issues, we must step up to consider the bigger picture. We observe **THE UNIVERSE** and **THE LAWS,** moving right along to learn about the workings of **CONSCIOUSNESS** and our **SENSE** of all there is. We have entered the mental realm of being.

Last but not least, we will take what we have learned and realize that **YOUR WORLD, INSIDE AND OUT,** is the same as cause and effect. Your innermost thoughts and convictions are reflected in your visible daily life's experiences.

So if we truly have the best interest in mind for ourselves and others, we will see how the **SPIDER EFFECT** ties it all together. All pieces of the puzzle will fall into place naturally.

Let's begin!

CHAPTER 1

MENTAL HOUSE CLEANING

Letting go and clearing your mind of the negative, life-denying stuff you have accumulated since birth is the first step.

> **"You cannot add to a vessel already full. First you must empty the contents, and then there will be room for the new."**
> *—William W. Walter*

Imagine returning your mind to its original state of health and clarity. Going back to easy, calm, playful, and pure thoughts like a child rather than feeling hectic and overloaded, as most of us experience in this extremely active world.

How?

Start in your home with a simple house cleaning. Empty your closets, drawers, and all your nooks and crannies—everything you've accumulated. It is

"...because you can!"

important to get rid of unnecessary items so you can begin to work through every area in your life.

Look at the "stuff" syndrome. Haven't we all moved stuff from one corner to another, or emptied out one closet just to pack it up and keep it in a box high up in the garage? Do you really know what's in your garage besides the car?

If you haven't used or worn it in three years, for crying out loud it's time to let it go. Why do you think storage units are such a big business? You are attached to stuff. The more you have, the more secure you feel and the richer you think you are. It's very personal.

The fact is that how you handle your stuff at home, at work, or in other areas of your life reflects your mental state. It is the visible picture of how clear or congested your thinking is.

Do you let things accumulate or are you organized? Are you a hoarder, or do you keep your home and workspace clean and neat? Is your thinking balanced and calm, or is it all over the place? Is your thinking clogged and your mind full to the brim with no room for focus?

In this process of letting go physically and mentally, you have to come up with a game plan to clear your home and your mind from unnecessary debris and old, outworn things and thoughts. Do you see the connection? Maybe you and a friend can organize a garage sale. You'll be surprised how many people are happily taking advantage of getting things for less. It'll be fun hanging out with friends and, at the end of the day you'll have a couple of dollars to treat yourself to an enjoyable outing at your favorite restaurant.

You can also donate those items that you don't use or require anymore (don't cling and don't make excuses) to a needy person or a charity. There are many ways of getting rid of stuff short of throwing them into the trash.

> **"I've come to believe that all my past failure and frustrations were actually laying the foundation for the understandings that have created the new level of living I now enjoy."**
> *—Tony Robbins*

We have established that a cluttered home is a cluttered Mind, and an organized home is an organized Mind. As with everything in life, it's easier to start with simple tasks first, like the house cleaning example. After you have accomplished the task, you will feel light and inspired, ready to revamp your life, ready to improve your surroundings. It will set the stage, allowing you to tackle a major mental makeover.

Once you have mastered "getting rid of stuff," it will be easier to finish cleaning and reorganizing the items you kept. Remember that your home should have the quality of ease and comfort. It symbolizes and reflects your state of mind. It should be relaxing, comfortable, peaceful, and quiet at times so you can meditate and enjoy.

As you develop your haven at home, you will feel a wave of mental easiness coming over you,

"...because you can!"

a lightening of the load, so to speak. It doesn't take a lot of money to create this type of environment. It takes only love and caring and a little imagination.

We are individuals, and we are unique. We all have a different sense of what is comforting, soothing, and attractive. It is good that we are diverse and have different, unique likes and ideas of what a true home should look like.

As long as you are happy and it makes you feel good, once your home has become your paradise, you have a winner.

> **"Glorify who you are today, do not condemn who you were yesterday, and dream of who you can be tomorrow."**
> **—Neale Donald Walsch**

Tackling the "stuff" to do

What about your to-do list? Let's say it seems that you have a million things on your agenda, just more stuff to attend to. The truth is that many of those items could be eliminated, or at least lessened, if you really think about it.

Do you really have to run to five different stores every weekend? Do you need all the stuff you buy? Is it vital that you plan an on-going agenda of social activities instead of creating some quiet time for yourself? Is it absolutely essential that you tend to the demands of family and friends every time they call? Are you having a problem saying no because you have the need to feel needed? Are you one of those people who come to the rescue of an old boyfriend or girlfriend even though he or she is dating someone else?

Yes, we will talk about tackling your imbalanced to-do list as well.

> **"God gave us the gift of life; it is up to us to give ourselves the gift of living well."**
> **—*Voltaire***

It's time to balance and reflect

The main goal here is to focus on you, your world, and your environment. After all, this is *your* life.

Your questions to yourself should be as follows: What are the corrections that need to be addressed and what areas of my thoughts and feelings need a mental makeover? What are the beliefs and concepts that I can clean out and no longer give attention to? What are the character traits that I need to improve? What are the thought habits that I can alter, and what are the emotions that need tending to?

> **"I never see what has been done; I only see what remains to be done."**
> **—*Buddha***

"...because you can!"

Do you want to learn principles you can use daily to live the life you want?

If you are ready to take charge of your life, this concept of better living that we are addressing is for you. The purpose of this book is to give you guidance and support in developing simple, daily practices for controlling, adjusting, and reworking your thoughts, emotions, and reactions. It will gently nudge you forward and point you in the right direction.

Through self-knowledge you can discover how intentionally right, good, loving thoughts, and actions help you to live more fully, abundantly, and happily.

Discover a new, creative approach to your life that is free of clutter; and by cleaning out your mental storage room, your newly found breathing room will show you how powerful you can become using your thoughts by right application.

You are finding out that there is a power that can transform your life. This power is not a mystery or something unattainable. It is right here within you, and you will be able to go beyond all limits and learn to create the life you desire. Cleaning out your physical and mental household is only the first step, but it is certainly a step in the right direction.

> **"If my mind can conceive it, and my heart can believe it, I know I can achieve it."**
> **—Jesse Jackson**

During this cleaning out process, you should go diligently on your way thinking happy and positive thoughts, making an effort to eliminate as much negativity as possible.

Although it seems negativity is everywhere you look, you must stand firm in not allowing this to influence or bother you.

You must learn to disregard the negative information that bombards you, especially that which comes through the media. Don't buy into the negative propaganda. Don't pay attention to others' mistakes and pessimism. Focus on your own misunderstandings, your own mistakes, and your own negative beliefs.

The truth is that Life is good, it is fair, and it has limitless possibilities. You deserve all the good there is. You deserve the best!

So let's move on to the next step—just like life itself—always moving forward and upward is our goal.

"The components of anxiety, stress, fear, and anger do not exist independently of you in the world. They simply do not exist in the physical world, even though we talk about them as if they do."
—*Wayne Dyer*

Are you ready to take the next step to better living?

Now that you have finished cleaning your home and have begun to clean your mental household,

"...because you can!"

you first must let go of old, outgrown, negative thoughts and concepts and make room for new and improved ideas.

Such unfulfilling thoughts that need to be discarded include hurry, worry, annoyance and agitation, pettiness, and any vague feeling of unease or discomfort. You need to look at all wrong thoughts, not only the obvious ones like anger and hate.

We humans have a daily thought pattern, a habit you might say, that we have acquired over a long time.

One thought pattern might consist of constant worry. No matter how good the day starts out, you will find something to worry about. Let's look at some examples.

Let's say you're on your way to the office and you worry about being stuck in traffic and late for work. You move on to worrying about the new client or deal you are trying to close. You worry about your kids and their safety while in school, and you're concerned about their bus ride home and the stranger they might encounter. You worry about dinner and homework. You worry about your husband or wife feeling neglected. This is just one simple example out of many daily experiences, so imagine all there is to worry about. Or is there?

Thought patterns are dangerous only because you are no longer conscious of how your moods change. The alterations are that subtle. It's like eating or breathing; it just happens without your consciousness being aware of it. Repetition will intensify the patterns and, just like any addiction, it becomes harder to break and correct.

> **"It's the repetition of affirmations that leads to belief. And once that belief becomes a deep conviction, things begin to happen."**
> **—Muhammad Ali**

Focus on balancing your life

Balance is the key to life. Your day should consist of part work, part play, part rest, and part meaningful contemplation, as W. W. Walter so eloquently stated. Your welfare should be at the top of the list.

To achieve this formula, see your work as an expression of your talents that you are happily contributing to the world. Be playful and lighthearted, rest easily with a clear conscience and spend time in quiet solitude to replenish your mind, contemplate new ideas, and reflect on the meaning of life.

Love and respect yourself by treating yourself well, by enjoying yourself, and by having genuine affection for your surroundings and your environment. Show appreciation for what you have and who you are. Purify your thoughts, and implement a healthy lifestyle.

Starting and maintaining a clean and pure life doesn't mean you have to stop all that you have considered to be fun up to now. You can enjoy the same

"...because you can!"

rhythm & blues and the same carefree amusement, but exercise moderation. Just listen to your heart—you know what to do.

Get that balance in check!

Other important areas need serious attention and clean-up, but we will address those areas in a later chapter. One is the eradication of fear. You will have to work diligently emptying out all your fears, small and large. There is a lifetime of accumulated stuff inside of you that needs to be sent to the cleaners!

> **"Happiness is not a matter of intensity but of balance, order, rhythm and harmony."**
> **—*Thomas Merton***

Include other people in your mental workout

There are and always will be "others" in your experience. Some are here for you to learn from, some are here to reflect or mirror some of your own qualities, and some are here to show you the necessary corrections needed in self.

Then, there are your loved ones that you have to deal with on a more emotional level. Those we call "others" are always connected to you in some way and are a mirror of your state of consciousness.

Be kind to everyone you come into contact with. Love thy neighbor as thyself. This doesn't mean that you have to associate with every person you meet, nor does it mean you have to hang out with people who may be unpleasant and alienating.

It means that you should feel compassion and love, knowing that they are also a part of the Universal source, and they, too, will eventually find the way. Send them your good and kind thoughts, and walk away tending to your own business.

In regard to the more unpleasant experiences you encounter, forgive and forget all hurts and emotional injuries that you believe have been inflicted upon you.

I know that ridding yourself of past hurts, resentments, and grudges is a daunting task. We all have been in situations when someone has done us wrong, or so we thought. We get mad, upset, offended, and disappointed. We think we have the right to feel the way we feel.

Your daily chore should be, as with cleaning out your house, to empty out old habits that include the way you think about others. Empty out traces of pettiness, criticism, jealousy, and sarcasm, and, instead, bring in loving thoughts, consideration, gentleness, and generosity. Let go of the grudges and resentments. Free yourself of the bondage of emotional pain.

Say to yourself, "I will practice kindness and non-judgment. I will begin my day with the statement, 'Today, I will be kind to everyone, and I will not judge anyone,'" and throughout the day remind yourself to stay on course.

"Beginning today, treat everyone you meet as if they were going to be dead by midnight. Extend to them all the care, kindness and understanding you can muster, and do it with no thought of any reward. Your life will never be the same again."
—*Og Mandino*

Everyone has a different viewpoint

There are different perspectives and always two sides to every story. At times we get involved in unpleasant confrontations or uncomfortable situations through no fault of our own.

Instead of reacting, we must take a step back and see these situations without any emotional or personal connection and feeling. I know it's not easy to look at this from a detached point of view, but it is necessary in order to make the correction.

It also seems that someone else, something outside of you has inflicted emotional wounds onto you. But ask yourself, who has really done those things to you? Haven't you allowed them to affect you? Have you accepted the insult as true? Have you acknowledged a stranger's statement as fact?

Speaking from a mental viewpoint, can someone really hurt you unless you react to it and believe they can injure you? Aren't you the one that thinks and feels hurt about the things said or done? Are you taking responsibility for your reactions and feelings?

Each of us reacts differently to certain situations. We perceive uniquely.

As an extreme example, let's say someone calls you "ugly." You might be very upset about the rudeness and insensitivity this individual displayed. If you are very insecure about yourself and your appearance, you might suffer severe self- doubt and feel a great lack of confidence.

If you, however, are a very secure person who knows who you are, you might laugh it off and go on with your business totally ignoring the affront, proving that it is not in the power of others to hurt you.

I am reiterating that no one can emotionally *hurt* or *disappoint* you but yourself.

Cleaning out your emotional hurts can be an excruciating task, but it has to be accomplished in order to move forward. You will be singing songs of joy; you will be free and ready for true enjoyment.

Reflect.

"Your living is determined not so much by what life brings to you as by the attitude you bring to life; not so much by what happens to you as by the way your mind looks at what happens."
—*Khalil Gibran*

Maybe it's you?

Maybe you're the one judging others and expecting them to act a certain way just because "that's what you would do." Are you the one getting annoyed with someone's behavior? Are you insensitive at times? Now who is being critical and judgmental?

Isn't it more than fair to let others be their own individuals, the designers of their own lives? Isn't it time to clean out your mind from all critical and judgmental thoughts? Think about how quickly and how often we judge other people.

You see someone walk down the street and you criticize their clothing, style of walking, or tone of voice. Or your co-worker annoys you with gossip, and you think he or she is petty and a rumormonger. Aren't those judgmental thoughts?

Yes, of course, there are certain people who are likeable and easy to love, but there are also some that are difficult or unpleasant to be around. But associating with them is a choice. If it's a workplace situation, and you cannot walk away from offensive co-workers or bosses, then make an effort not to take criticism or judgments personally. Leave the room without reacting or feeling uneasy. If you can help it, do not personally react and feel about them or their behavior at all.

Because feeling is an instant reaction, it's more difficult to control, and it will take practice. But once you have mastered the art of feeling, you will be in charge of a much better emotional energy. Feeling correctly can be acquired through right thinking.

These points are not being brought to your attention to put you down or criticize you. It has to be emphasized so you will realize that we all think, act, and feel many times unconsciously, due to habits of thinking that we have acquired over a lifetime.

A friend of mine just told me the story of how an associate of his wrote a "Dear John" letter that included current issues and unresolved feelings. He then mailed it to himself. He stepped away from his personal feelings and wrote the letter as though it were meant for a friend.

It is a great exercise and you should try it. Be honest, no matter how painful. Once the letter arrives at your doorstep, you will see your woes in a totally new light. Use this tool to step away from a personal sense that usually affects our judgment.

"The fact is that people are good; Give people affection and security, and they will give affection and be secure in their feelings and their behavior."
—Abraham Maslow

Yes, the fact is, all people are naturally good. In reality, all people are of the same substance, which is Universal goodness, Intelligence, or good quality. Being of the same substance means they are as precious as you are.

"...because you can!"

Keep this in mind if they act improperly or if it looks like they are not of good character. Just because they are behaving badly does not mean they are inherently bad.

You must always separate the individual (their Soul or true Spirit) from their behavior and their actions. Their upbringing has molded them into who they are. "If they would know better, they would do better" as one of my teachers used to say a long time ago. It has stuck with me.

Yes, they also have a choice. They also can change their lives, but it is up to them to do so. You can only take care of yourself. You are the thinker and creator of your own world, and by your own betterment you will positively affect everyone with whom you come into contact.

You will be a healing force in the Universe as you are part of the Allness of Life.

This is the beginning of your journey to a better, happier Life.

Put your walking shoes on, and let's walk the talk... because you can!

ANSWER THESE QUESTIONS HONESTLY:

1. Do you let things accumulate or are you organized? What does it reflect?
2. Is your thinking calm and balanced, or is it fluttered, clogged, and full to the brim with no room for focus?
3. Do you need all the stuff you buy, and do you overfill your social calendar? Would you be satisfied with less material stuff and greater mental ease?
4. What character trait needs improvement? What are your weaknesses? What are your strengths?
5. What are the thought habits you need to change?
6. Have you allowed others to affect you? Why?
7. Are you sometimes critical and judgmental, and do you want to work on changing your demeanor?
8. Can you step away from taking things so personally?
9. Can you accept the fact that all people are good no matter what their behavior exhibits?
10. Are you willing to change your thinking? Are you ready to clean out the clutter?

CHAPTER 2

BELIEFS

"Beliefs have the power to create and the power to destroy. Human beings have the awesome ability to take any experience of their lives and create a meaning that disempowers them or one that can literally save their lives."
—*Tony Robbins*

A belief is usually an absolute conviction or acceptance of something you think is right or true. It does not mean that it is the truth; you only think it is.

Here are some of the basic beliefs we have to empty out before we can gain a deeper insight into the working of the Laws of Life. We will discuss many of the issues as we go along on this voyage together.

Beliefs that need special attention

Are we humans material beings?

"...because you can!"

Most of us are aware—and scientists have confirmed—that our bodies are composed of energy, not matter. This scientific fact has to be understood deeply by each of us in order to see the positive effects the body will express when this truth is realized. It will shed a new light on our beliefs of health, overall well-being, aging, and death. It changes everything.

Our work is to destroy the belief that our body is solid. We are Spirit. We are Soul. We are Consciousness. We are perfect Intelligence. All of these characteristics are mental. Our body is only a visible reflection of our thinking. We are what we think.

> **"Spirit is the real and eternal; matter is the unreal and temporal."**
> **—Mary Baker Eddy**

What do so-called material things consist of?

Things are "thinks." They are thoughts objectified.

Anything that we see in the visible world was once only an idea or someone's thought or concept. All is mental in origin and, like our bodies, made of energy. Each object has a different density but, broken down as scientists have demonstrated the objects we see are ideas brought into the visible, or thoughts made manifest.

Gerald L. Schroeder is a scientist, author, and lecturer who focuses on what he perceives to be an inherent relationship between science and spirituality. In his book *The Science of God,* he points out the following:

> **"Changing one's paradigm is not easy. Millennia passed before humankind discovered that energy is the basis of matter. It may take a few more years before we prove that wisdom and knowledge are the basis of—and can actually create—energy, which in turn creates matter."**
> *—Gerald L. Schroeder*

In practical terms, the touchable items we use daily are made for our convenience and enjoyment on this plane. They are mental in concept, yet they have been created for a purpose.

Just ask yourself what is the function of the simple things you use on a daily basis. A cup is here to drink out of, a car for driving, and a stove to cook on. Everything is a symbol of something in the unseen. It was conceived in the mental realm. It was invented by someone's thoughts and ideas to serve a function and be of service. It was manifested through their creative thought power for us to enjoy.

Belief in matter is a purely human belief and must be eradicated completely. This must be done through careful reasoning. No matter what the appearance, the fact remains there aren't any physical conditions.

Without your mentality, there would be no recognition, no action, no feeling; all would be void.

"...because you can!"

The outer conditions of a person's life will always be found to reflect their inner beliefs.
—James Lane Allen

Your mind's connection to Wellness

A "sound mind is a sound body" means more than being sane as commonly perceived. Mind and mind healing are of utmost importance, and I have included an overview in the Well-being chapter.

Today, many health problems have been attributed to unhealthful living and stress, which are of mental origin. We have started to make the Mind/body connection.

I understand too well that anyone afflicted by a disease or illness is inclined to disagree with the statement that the illness or discomfort experienced is mostly self-induced.

Stay open-minded and let it simmer in your consciousness before you dismiss those ideas or judge them as nonsense. As we know, all new ideas are met with resistance and require some careful "stewing" before being accepted.

Allow yourself to feel the truth. I am not asking you or anyone to blindly believe; rather, I am asking you to keep an open mind. Apply what you learn daily. Study the principles given and test them for yourself. The results will speak for themselves and, with this newfound faith; your beliefs will turn into useable knowledge and understanding. This knowledge, in turn, will be your savior.

This might be the first time you've heard that physical sickness and one's mental attitude are intertwined. Maybe you are already familiar with this idea and are working on improving your mental and physical health. However, you may or may not *want to* recognize yourself as the source of your illnesses.

You will eventually have to take this responsibility, or you will not be in the driver's seat; you will be a victim for life. What I want is for you to be the driver of your destiny.

Sickness and Well-being, like everything else in life, are purely mental. The connection of a sound mind and a sound body is cause and effect in action. Any sickness you experience is the effect of your sick or wrong habitual, uneasy thinking, with fear being the biggest tormenter.

There is no self-blame intended in this statement. You have been living without this awareness up to this point. But now is the time to change your thoughts, beliefs, habits, and daily actions to reflect a healthier you.

Although it's true that some diseases and ailments are more difficult to heal, especially the chronic and longstanding ones that you have had as long as you can remember, it is not too late. Any betterment is better than none. Any relief of pain and suffering is a blessing brought on by you and your new and improved thinking.

> **"Acknowledging the good that you already have in your life is the foundation for all abundance."**
> —*Eckhart Tolle*

Acknowledging any and all good you already have is the foundation of all the blessings you experience including health, wealth, and happiness.

Beliefs that should be tossed in the garbage bin

Belief in Poverty:

We are talking not just about a lack of material riches, but also about spiritual poverty.

In reality, abundance is our birthright. However, many people are seemingly born into great material hardship and scarcity.

The absence of abundance in so many people's lives is a visible picture of the dearth in their mentality of a sense of wealth. They are missing the sense of self-sufficiency. They feel less than, unworthy, out of luck, left out, not good enough, poor, and so forth.

Taking it to a personal level, you can change the appearance of poverty into wealth by finding out what abundance consists of. By providing the necessary thought corrections in a step-by-step manner, you will acquire wealth consciousness. This will be logically explained in the Abundance chapter.

Spiritual poverty has nothing to do with worldly riches. It is a lack of love and an inability to be the best you can be. It is a shortage of compassion, honesty, sincerity, and your responsibility to yourself as a creator. It is also a lack of interest and indifference to all humankind and to this planet we call our home.

Wealth is within us; poverty is a sickness or deficiency. Poverty or hardship is unnatural and needs mental healing.

Your belief in poverty, even if you think you are born into this lifestyle, is what's making you poor, and your sense of inferiority and low self-esteem is what's keeping you suppressed.

Your fears and doubts are holding you in bondage and are preventing you from growth and a happy and blissful life. But you are never defeated unless you give up.

In addition to worries about poverty, we have to acknowledge the mental monster called fear.

"The whole secret of existence is to have no fear. Never fear what will become of you, depend on no one. Only the moment you reject all help are you freed."
—Buddha

"...because you can!"

You cannot function with fear looking over your shoulder, so whatever it is that you are afraid of has to be honestly examined and resolved. Why are you doing what you are doing? Are you afraid of failure? Are you terrified of change?

Tell yourself over and over again that you have talents and you have services that you can provide to others that are needed and cherished. You are creative, so use your imagination and, most of all, develop courage to face your challenges, and embrace your opportunities.

Do this daily and believe it with all of your heart and soul.

Like all other areas in your life, this also involves spiritual healing and house cleaning. I'm going back to the principle that a clean house is a clean mind, and poverty does not belong there. It is your mind that causes abundance or poverty, so why not choose the better one of the two?

Empty out your belief in poverty, and let in the sunlight of your mind!

> **"Write it on your heart that every day is the best day in the year."**
> **—*Ralph Waldo Emerson***

Look at the end of the tunnel. There is a way out!

We've heard great stories of individuals having worked their way up from an unimaginable, impoverished background like Oprah, whose life as everyone knows is very inspiring. John Paul DeJoria, who is worth about $4 billion, is another good example.

Ever heard the name Paul Mitchell, the co-founder of a popular brand of hair products? He once sold newspapers to help support his single mother, who later sent him to foster care when she could no longer support him. Homeless for a time, living in his car, and pushing hair care products door-to-door...and the rest is history.

J. K. Rowling is another example of great courage and determination. She is the author of the Harry Potter books and movie series. While writing wizardry in a pub on napkins, the single mother lived on welfare in Edinburgh, Scotland. Broke and depressed the author once told reporters she contemplated suicide. Her book was published in 1997 and quickly became a bestseller. It was the first of a seven-book series that captivated children and adults worldwide.

The list of people that overcame impoverished circumstances is long, and the examples mentioned are huge successes. Some of you will think that those were lucky breaks. Maybe you think you do not have the talents that these people have, but there are many other stories from regular, everyday people like myself.

Born in a small village in Austria shortly after World War II, my family lived in two tiny rooms with no running water, no refrigeration, and, of course, no TV. Perishables had to be stored on the windowsill; there

"...because you can!"

was cold running water only in the common area and a toilet down the hall for four families to share.

We children played with sticks and blankets and would go into the woods where we "built" imaginary places out of the moss growing on the stately trees of the forest. My father was a machinist and barely made enough to pay the bills. My mother helped by sewing and knitting my clothes and worked part time in a factory.

With the stress of the times and very little enjoyment in their relationship, they divorced by the time I was fifteen. My mother always told me, even when I was just a toddler, that I was "very smart" and kept instilling this sense in me over and over. I did well in school, but when it was time to go to a higher academy, the parents of the children that were "better off" than our family did not approve of my association with their offspring. I could have been devastated and could have believed that I was worth less than they were, unworthy, and that I was doomed to a meager life. But this was not what I accepted in my mind, nor what I wanted for my life.

I left the country soon thereafter, methodically carving out a meaningful life. It included travels to foreign countries, making music, and establishing new relationships that ultimately brought me to America where my career took off.

I was a seeker, fortunate and curious enough to find a "right thinking" sponsor shortly after my settling in Los Angeles and have been diligently pursuing this lifestyle ever since.

Just looking around, I see many friends and family that have overcome great obstacles of so-called poverty as well and are enjoying a blessed life through their effort, courage, and determination.

"Abundance is not something we acquire. It is something we tune into."
—Wayne Dyer

What about the evil you see?

You believe that the evil you see is real through believing your five senses and assuming that what you see, hear, touch, smell, or taste is fact. You are prone to believe evil exists as you watch events unfold around the world: wars, gang activities, drugs, kidnappings, and murders, all of which look mighty real from a human standpoint.

However, bad or evil events are not real. They are man-made. You have to start seeing the difference. Every evil occurrence you see or experience was made by someone's evil or malicious intent. Wickedness is a distorted sense or lack of good feeling.

No matter what the appearance, the fact remains that in reality there is nothing bad about life and this Universe. The Universe and Infinite Intelligence, which are one and the same, on a spiritual level are perfect—pure and good by nature.

Intelligence can only act intelligently or it would not be intelligent. Perfection can only act perfectly, and so on. Evil is the opposite of good and therefore cannot be true or real. It is an ever-so-unpleasant illusion.

If I'm losing you, stay with me. I will explain much more in later chapters. Remember we are only emptying out many beliefs right now. We will go through it step by step and reason extensively until we are as clear as a whistle.

> **"Love is the only reality and it is not a mere sentiment. It is the ultimate truth that lies at the heart of creation."**
> *—Rabindranath Tagore*

Let's throw out the belief in old age, decay, and death

You are a soul that lives forever and will, when the time of your passing comes, experience only a change of awareness. For now be assured that you are only maturing, which is a good thing and, therefore, your sense of aging has to change to a more positive and youthful outlook.

The body, as scientifically proven, renews itself constantly. As Deepak Chopra—one of several physicians and scientists with the same conclusions—points out in his book *The Higher Self* published in 1993 that our bodies renew themselves constantly: stomach cells renew every five days; skin cells are replaced every month; the skeleton is replaced every three months; the raw material of DNA is replaced every six weeks; and our brain cells are completely new every year.

The whole body is replaced every two years, which supports Chopra's notion that the essence of the self is "timeless."

Some people age much more quickly than others. I am sure this is due to the individual's mental belief about aging. How else could it be? Your physical substance of your body at the time of death, according to those studies, would be only about two years old.

**"Time is not measured by the passing of years
but by what one does, what one feels,
and what one achieves."
—*Jawaharlal Nehru***

Staying youthful means staying active, involved, and, most of all, being interested in Life itself. Continue to be enthusiastic and love to live. Your natural vim and vigor will keep you young. Learning keeps you fresh; shutting down without interest in the new, on the other hand, will age you.

You were born to unfold and gain an Understanding of the principles of life so you can move higher and higher up in the scale of being. Progressing through life has nothing to do with physical aging. It has everything to do with mental maturity, which is forever young.

At the time of death or passing, we leave the so-called material body behind, proving that the body never had life of its own. Your body cannot think of itself. Consciousness thinks. Thinking is the activity of your Consciousness.

"...because you can!"

At the time of passing, your Soul or Consciousness goes on to experience another dimension of Life. Life cannot die; it would be the opposite. Life lives!

In order to gain an understanding of the Allness of Good and the principles we are addressing, you need only an immense desire and good common sense with a willingness to learn. This, coupled with an open mind, will get you there. You are here to unfold your innate perfection.

> **"The end of life is to be like God, and the soul following God will be like Him."**
> **—*Socrates***

Your connection to God

It is not my intent to take your God away, but I want you to better understand what God consists of and how God works. We have to find out what existed first in order to find God.

We know that Universal Consciousness, Intelligence, was first since without consciousness nothing could have been consciously recognized and, therefore, would have been void.

You are Consciousness; you are Life and therefore of the same substance and quality. You are also intelligent, giving you all of the same attributes that Universal substance and power has.

Beliefs

All metaphysical writers, past and present, have used Bible quotes and interpreted them beautifully, depending on their degree of understanding. It's all right there in this great book of wisdom; sadly enough, it is mostly misinterpreted.

At this point of your unfoldment, and especially since you are reading these pages, I am certain that your belief that a "person" as your "God" has been mostly eradicated.

I am not saying there is no God; rather, I am saying that we have to find out "what" God really is and his relationship to us.

Most of us can probably agree that God is not an old man that sits on a throne way up in the sky rewarding or punishing us to his heart's content.

We have also found that a personal God does not respond to our prayers. And why should he since it would mean that he prefers one human over the other? God is no respecter of persons; he does not decide who gets killed or wins the war, and he does not choose to take a child at birth or inflict pain. It would make him a monster.

I think we can agree that God is all good and that God is Spirit. It has been stated numerous times in the Bible, and our reason will confirm this theory. Spirit means mentality.

"...because you can!"

> **"Can you tell a plain man the road to heaven? Certainly, turn at once to the right, and then go straight forward."**
> —*William Wilberforce*

Bliss and Damnation

There are no far away places called heaven or hell; those are states of mind right here and now. You don't have to look far, and you don't have to go anywhere to experience heaven or hell.

Aren't you in heaven when your loved ones are next to you, your children are growing up beautifully, you've just gotten a promotion at work, or you're sipping a cocktail next to the pool on a wonderful, sunny day?

Aren't you in hell when you are depressed, you are full of pain and hurt, or when the creditors are knocking down your door because you can't afford to pay your bills?

Heaven and hell are created by us. You and I are the cause of all that befalls us every day of our lives. We are in charge, we are the makers, and we are creators. We love or hate, we conquer or fail, and we are at peace or at war. It is a lot of responsibility to accept this knowledge, but it is always our choice.

God, or whatever your name for "it" is, is an almighty good Universal power or substance, called Consciousness or Infinite Intelligence, of which we are a part.

When we find the All Power, the All Mighty Source of the Universe and its connection to each of us, we have found God.

> "...that which was first must have been the primal Cause or Creator...can you possibly discover anything which could have existed before Consciousness?"
> —*William W. Walter*

The Vital Error

One of humankind's vital errors is the belief that humans are one creation and God is another. We have separated "us" from "him." Understanding that we are One and the same—same as to substance (spirit, not material), quality (goodness) and quantity (perfection), same as to love and mental nature—will bring us to the starting point of all there is. Now, let's utilize this newfound power for our own good and all humanity.

> "Dear God, Please send to me the spirit of your peace. Then send, dear Lord, the spirit of peace from me to all the world. Amen."
> —*Marianne Williamson*

What helps during this process?

Surround yourself with like-minded people. Enjoy your family and friends. Enjoy yourself. Keep interested in beauty and vital activities that enrich your life.

"...because you can!"

As we know now, like attracts like. Churches and organizations are crutches, and it's okay if that's where you are at this point and you feel it's what you need right now. However, their leaders are still giving power to outside forces, and you will have to learn that you are the arbiter of your own fate.

No one can do it for you, so let go of the crutches and start walking the path on your own. You can do it!

"Don't go around saying the world owes you a living. The world owes you nothing. It was here first."
—Mark Twain

Lift your thoughts to a higher sense about old beliefs and embrace the new

Intellectuality is not Intelligence. Most intellectuals are actually handicapped by the belief that they have a great deal of knowledge and, therefore, know more than the average person. They are less willing to be open-minded and will not accept the Truth as easily as an open-minded individual would.

You must first recognize the error in your thought, acknowledge the mistake, and accept that correction is needed, which can only be accomplished through complete honesty. Then you will have room in your Mind for the new and will listen to the truth that will change your life. The Truth about anything, not just Universal Truth, is always mental; it always starts in your mind. Truth is the knowing of actuality and the natural workings of the Universe, which is composed of the Laws.

The workings of your mind are an individualized reflection of this process. The reality is that your mind produces ideas; those ideas find expressions through your thought convictions. Ideas must take on shape or we would not be able to differentiate one idea from another on this plane.

Thought is the power by which we bring into visibility that which is invisible. It always starts in the invisible realm.

Hopefully, we will bring ideas into the visible that are beneficial to our enjoyment, ideas that create a better life. When we understand the mental process, we will be able to follow the different states of mental activities on any specific problem. We will be able to apply the same Laws and processes to each problem, which makes it simple. Life is simple.

"One must marry one's feelings to one's beliefs and ideas. That is probably the only way to achieve a measure of harmony in one's life."
—*Napoleon Hill*

So to reiterate, to begin we have to get rid of the old beliefs and ideas and replace them with new and improved desires. As your mentality is always in a state of creative motion, it is ready to express your convictions at any time.

Go ahead and empty out and replace each area of your daily experience with happy, healthy, and abundant thoughts and desires. Your experience will be marvelous...because you can!

ANSWER THESE QUESTIONS HONESTLY:

1. Do you believe that humans are material beings? What about things? Are they material? Write down your best sense about this subject.
2. Do you believe that your wellness is connected with your state of mind?
3. Why are you doing what you are doing? Do you want to change the way you live and feel? Or are you happy and content?
4. Are you afraid of change or do you embrace the new? Are you afraid of failure? Why?
5. Can you see that poverty is a state of mind and that it can be corrected?
6. Do you believe the evil you see around you is real?
7. Are you afraid of getting old and frail? Do you believe it is your destiny?
8. What does God mean to you?
9. The vital error of thinking that we are one thing and God is another accounts for most of our suffering. Can you accept the fact that we are one and the same with God?
10. What will help you to get rid of the old beliefs? Are you willing to take the necessary steps?

CHAPTER 3

HAPPINESS

"Trust yourself. Create the kind of self that you will be happy to live with all your life. Make the most of yourself by fanning the tiny, inner sparks of possibility into flames of achievement."
—Golda Meir

Make Happiness Your Goal!

When you make happiness your goal, you will easily accomplish what you desire because happiness is a natural state of mind, and it is a positive force in the creation process. Happiness is a high mental frequency; it is a state of fulfillment and joy.

Ask yourself, "What makes me happy?"

At first, you might list material things: money, a new car, a new house, some exotic vacation, or expensive jewelry. But such possessions are elusive. They will not last forever, nor are they the source of true happiness.

"...because you can!"

Then there are the less tangible desires: You might want love and a loving relationship. Maybe you want more time to yourself. Or you desire greater status and respect. There are countless ways we attempt to make ourselves happy.

Remember that nothing or no one outside of yourself can make you experience pure happiness. Happiness comes from within, from your innermost blissful thought habits and convictions, your sense of self-worth, self-sufficiency, and from your self-love.

Happiness should be a well-rounded sense of contentment and bliss. Some might call it Grace.

No doubt that you should have *all* the material things you want. They are here for you to enjoy, but don't make them your prime focus. They are a natural outcome provided by your right inner mental attitude and will be added to your experience automatically as your sense improves.

"Happiness is the reward we get for living to the highest right we know."
—Richard Bach

So live the highest "right" you know!

Happiness should include all areas of your life such as the people around you and your environment.

Consider these questions: Do you cherish your family and friends and are you happy around them? Do you enjoy the home in which you live? Does observing nature make you feel alive? Do you spend time looking at the skies? Do you feel blessed because you are healthy? Are you grateful for your youthful attitude and overall well-being?

When do you feel the happiest?

You have to ask these questions because the most important task in your life is to get in touch with your inner self: your source, your strength, your power. Your world is about you; therefore, you must understand yourself first "and all things will be added unto you." When you are transformed, your world is transformed because you and your world are One and the same.

"Life is full of beauty. Notice it. Notice the bumble bee, the small child, and the smiling faces. Smell the rain, and feel the wind. Live your life to the fullest potential, and fight for your dreams."
—*Ashley Smith*

Like attracts like, happiness begets happiness

There was an interesting segment on *60 Minutes*, a popular news show. Research showed the "happiest town" and the "unhappiest town" in the United States.

The "City of Happiness" was Boulder, Colorado, where people live a healthy lifestyle and enjoy their daily activities. The "City of Despair" was Huntington, West Virginia, and was named the unhealthiest city by the *Huffington Post*. What made these places so different from each other were the people and their

"...because you can!"

general attitude. Groups of people are drawn to each other in certain places by status, healthy eating habits, exercise, enjoyment of beautiful things, and a positive outlook of life, whereas others see themselves as lacking, hopeless, and prone to unhealthy and negative expectations.

The City of Boulder, with active families and seniors, has the healthiest population of people who are outdoors-oriented, people who enjoy their daily lives and exhibit happy, contented dispositions.

On the other side of the spectrum, the people in Huntington were smoking, drinking, eating unhealthy foods, becoming overweight, and were battling all kinds of other addictions. The most important difference was that they called themselves unhappy.

Here is an excerpt from the *Huffington Post* article:

A report issued by the Centers for Disease Control August 15, 2008, using survey data from 2006, reported that Huntington is among the unhealthiest cities in America. The survey found that 24.3% of adults 18 years-of-age or older reported themselves as in poor to fair health. The survey also found that 48.1% of residents over 65 years of age in the Huntington-Ashland, West Virginia-Kentucky-Ohio statistical area had all their natural teeth extracted. In addition, the CDC reports that 45.5% of adults over the age of 20 years are obese. 21.6% of adults over 45 years of age reported a diagnosis of coronary heart disease while another 12.7% of adults aged 18 or older reported a diagnosis of diabetes. An Associated Press article describes lifestyle and cultural barriers as obstacles to better public health. As examples, the article describes local eating habits (the number of pizza shops in Huntington alone exceeding the total number of health clubs available in the entire state of West Virginia), the relatively sedentary culture, and poor education as causes for health issues described in the CDC report. In an MSNBC report published November 16, 2008, Huntington was rated as the unhealthiest city in the United States. The study took into consideration obesity rates, toothlessness and levels of healthcare.

As a consequence of Huntington's high rates of obesity, diabetes and coronary heart disease, Huntington was selected by Jamie Oliver to be the location of his television series, Jamie Oliver's Food Revolution.

Mind you, all of the residents interviewed by *60 Minutes* in this survey in each respective city were blue-collar workers with similar backgrounds. Most significantly, there existed no "good fortune," "luck," or "born into wealth" as a contributing factor to account for the differences in attitude toward life and in the people's experiences.

We create our own reality. We are drawn to similar people, similar surroundings, similar interests, and similar cultural and political beliefs.

We are a mirror reflecting ourselves. So if it appears that you don't enjoy your reality, you must change your inner sense, and your world will alter accordingly to reflect your new inner being.

"...because you can!"

This process of unfoldment goes on forever, and you will gain a better and greater picture as your awareness of the Allness of Good improves. Again, think of your life as a mirror reflecting back your thoughts, convictions, beliefs, and feelings.

"The primary cause of unhappiness is never the situation but your thoughts about it."
—*Eckhart Tolle*

Stay positively active and create a happy environment

It is the nature of the Soul to move forward and upward and, therefore, your experiences will sometimes reflect greater challenges, obstacles, and tests to keep you in motion. Not all of them are positive. You might encounter unpleasantness and pain if you are stagnant, but you will be shoved forward through those challenges.

If you are active and grow through your own doing, learning your lessons along the way, those challenges will lessen and you will live a calmer, happier, more peaceful life. By doing so, you are naturally flowing and working with the Universal current. You are not fighting against yourself.

We need to constantly expand and learn in order to stay stimulated. So pick up a new hobby, read more, learn a new trade, start a new career that you have dreamt about for a long time, or go to school to improve what you are doing right now. Start whatever you think will make you happy. Have the courage for change!

> **"You must be the change you wish
> to see in the world."**
> *—Mohandas Gandhi*

You cannot sit idle and expect things to change. Unless you start right now by changing your part of the world, it will continue to appear the same to you. Yes, you must be the change that you want your mental mirror to reflect back to you.

For years my job in the entertainment industry came first. While I raised a son and kept a household, I worked long hours thinking that I had to do this to "get somewhere." I justified it by saying that I really loved my job, which I did at the time. I was trapped in the belief that nothing was gained without hard labor.

I had studied metaphysics for many years and was a very devoted student. Deep down I knew that my unfoldment was more important in the grander scheme of life, and I realized that my existence had become imbalanced. I wasn't truly happy anymore, and it took honesty and courage to change my path.

I had to step out of my comfort zone. I had to dare to live my life differently. I had to walk the talk, practice what I preached, and put my money where my mouth was. Today I can say it was well worth it.

Why is reading, meditating, and studying your *Life* necessary?

When you are studying a mental science and working with the Laws, it's helpful to find a like-minded guide or group to share your thoughts and to help you stay on course. It's fun to exchange ideas, and it will prevent you from being stagnant or moving in the wrong direction. Don't "follow" any particular one; stay clear within your own mind and always listen to your heart.

If you do not have a like-minded group in your area, set regular time aside for your reading and contemplating the materials. There are many good books and websites available for anyone who is seriously searching.

"Go beyond science, into the region of metaphysics. Real religion is beyond argument. It can only be lived both inwardly and outwardly."
—*Swami Sivananda*

What challenges come up in your daily life? What are these lessons about?

The lessons are about you, your life, your health, your abundance, your relationships, your work, and your progress in unfoldment. They are here to show you what needs to be improved as it is all about you and your connection to your world.

You will find out that you are the master of your life and that you can better yourself, your experiences, and your relationships with people starting right now. Not tomorrow, not next week—right now!

Your daily experiences demonstrate how important it is that you reconnect with the Almighty Source of the

Universe and live the best life you can imagine. What I mean by this is that you need to listen to your own innate Intelligence. You, your true essence, already knows all there is to know; you just have to become aware of your knowing. A commitment to diligent study and improving your thoughts will get you there.

Set time aside and devote yourself to making it your primary interest. *You* should be your first priority. *Your* happiness should be on top of the list. It will surely improve your overall well-being and change your everyday life for the better.

In this process of gaining more happiness, ask yourself the following questions and be honest: What is your mental attitude? Do you see the world as hostile or good? Are you in general an easy-going person? Do you like people, your co-workers, and even strangers, or are you distant and hostile to others? Do you just tolerate certain individuals or do you enjoy them? Are you a doer, a go getter or a procrastinator? Are you a victor or a victim, a positive or negative individual?

The materials taught and the questions asked, when answered honestly, will open your eyes, and with this better knowledge you will have the tools you need.

"Happy is he who can trace effects to their causes."
—*Virgil*

Another important lesson, as a student of the Laws of Mind, is to cease giving power to external causes.

"...because you can!"

Letting go of making everything outside of yourself cause is a responsibility that cannot be taken lightly.

You will find that knowing what you want will cause your conscious mind to carry out your desire. This makes your thought, the activity of your consciousness, cause. It will bring your ideas into the visible world because you have a definite concept in your mind of what you want or wish to acquire for your happiness.

You will experience the strong awakening of having an inner creative power, but first you must acquire a positive conviction that *it is so*. I can assure you that you will discover your powerful capabilities. Absorb the statement: "You are the cause of all that befalls you every day of your life."

You will awaken to the fact that you must love and be compassionate. You must embrace all people, love the animal kingdom, and love plant life and all of Nature because all of these things are Life itself. All of these contribute to Universal Happiness.

"Happiness is mental harmony; unhappiness is mental inharmony."
—James Allen

Prove "that you can" to yourself

With everything you prove to yourself, you gain a better understanding of how it works. With this better understanding, you automatically manifest a better experience, environment, life, and you will gain the power to exhibit anything you want, including happiness.

You will go to sleep feeling successful and totally satisfied with your day's work. Your last thoughts before you fall asleep should be those of contentment, happiness, and bliss. A grateful heart will guarantee you a good night's sleep. Leave worry and fear behind. Sleep is essential and invigorating. Let your body and mind rest so you can multiply your good peacefully the next day.

Wherever you go, and whoever you encounter, this new line of thought, when rightly applied, will begin the process of circulating joy and affluence in your life and in the lives of others you come into contact with.

Make a commitment to keep love circulating in your life by giving and receiving life's most precious gifts: caring, affection, appreciation, and love. Each time you meet someone, you silently wish them happiness, joy, and laughter. The results will be your proof that you are on the right path.

My writings are the thoughts of my path; I have proven the workings of my mind to myself many times. You have to find your own way. The end goal for everyone is always the same: perfect harmony, a peaceful life, comfort, and, most of all, love and happiness.

The purpose of Life is to enjoy. It really doesn't matter how you get there, as long as it is done with good intentions. If you have a sincere desire, you will accomplish your goal of happiness.

"...because you can!"

We are all connected, of the same source and same substance; yet, the key is that we are individuals. Therefore, you have to find what works best for you. I can write about my findings, my experiences, my ways, and, hopefully, you can benefit from them. But you have to do the work yourself.

Don't just believe what anyone says. Prove it to yourself over and over and over again until you know that you know that you know.

"Happiness doesn't depend on any external conditions; it is governed by our mental attitude."
—Dale Carnegie

Happiness also means learning to keep feelings in check

When situations and events arise that upset or disturb you, and you experience an emotional meltdown, pull yourself up quickly. It won't take much time if you view it as a learning experience rather than a disaster.

Everything that we have shoved under the rug, we need to eventually clean out. Now is the time. Procrastination never works. Feelings are tougher to control as they seem to be more personal.

I always liked Karol K. Truman's tagline "Feelings buried alive never die..." In other words, no matter what you say or think, unless you have corrected your feelings, including how you feel about someone or something, nothing will change.

Since in the mental, *feeling* is the "mother" or "womb" of all expressions or manifestations and gives birth to all there is, it is imperative to keep your feelings right. You will always express or manifest the essence of your feelings. No matter how much you have reasoned about the subject, and you might be very well versed in this exercise, you will not get the desired results unless you have corrected your feelings about the subject matter.

Happiness is a feeling.

When you look at the lives of friends and family, you might see similar life patterns in their experiences.

You can now, as an Understander, diagnose their thought outline and mind model through their visible happiness or woes and be supportive, if necessary. Please only respond to your observations if they ask for your help.

"All that we are is the result of what we have thought. If a man speaks or acts with an evil thought, pain follows him. If a man speaks or acts with a pure thought, happiness follows him, like a shadow that never leaves him."
—Buddha

Stop complaining about the happenings in the world

If you want more peace, live peacefully. If you want a more loving society, be more loving. If you want to stop poverty, be more generous. And if you want more happiness, be happy.

"...because you can!"

Each contribution, no matter how small, adds to and brings out the goodness that is inherent in all of us. Your gift of right thought has a ripple effect in the world.

We grow, evolve, and expand our consciousness on a daily basis in degrees of our Understanding. Individually and collectively we will gain greater awareness in infinity.

We are in the midst of conscious evolution, and we have an opportunity to contribute to the transformation of life on the planet. Our old, outgrown thoughts sometimes feel safe and so we continue the same way, like sitting in an old, worn armchair. We subconsciously hold on to the familiar feelings.

We as individuals must progress and renew our outlooks and convictions to catch up with life's progress and unfoldment. We must not stay stagnant and tremor with fear.

We have to muster up our courage and move forward, each of us contributing to a better and happier place we call this world...because we can!

"I don't know what your destiny will be, but one thing I know: the only ones among you who will be really happy are those who will have sought and found how to serve."
—*Albert Schweitzer*

ANSWER THESE QUESTIONS HONESTLY:

1. What makes you happy?
2. Are you in general a happy person?
3. Do you enjoy the home you live in, the people you know, and the surroundings you deal with every day?
4. Do you live a healthy lifestyle?
5. What challenges come up in your daily life? What tests do you have to tackle?
6. Is taking time to study a mental science and is reading inspirational books part of your daily routine?
7. What is your mental attitude? Are you a victor or a victim?
8. Are you ready to observe and heal your feelings?
9. Do you see the connection between reasoning and feeling? Do you see the difference?
10. Do you believe that "you can"?

CHAPTER 4

DESIRE, IMAGINATION, AND VISUALIZATION

What do you really want out of life?

"Desire is the starting point of all achievement, not a hope, not a wish, but a keen pulsating desire which transcends everything."
—Napoleon Hill

Indeed, desire is the starting point of all achievement, but most of all it is the starting point of imagination and the active spark or beginning of all creation.

What are your true desires? Are they in conformity with your Soul and not just wishes for material riches? What do you think will make you happy? What will make you a better person?

When people are asked what they would want if they could have anything, it is mostly a so-called material "thing." I'm saying "so-called material 'thing'"

"...because you can!"

because no-thing is material; everything is mental in its origin.

Maybe respondents want a new car, a new house, or a vacation in a tropical place. We all have our ideas of what we want and what would make us happy. There are more than enough options of all kinds of goods available these days to choose from.

Picture yourself walking around in a multi-leveled mall. There are so many choices, perhaps too many, and this overload entices you to focus on getting more "goods" instead of more spiritual value—the true good.

We live in an age when change occurs in micro milliseconds. The technology we bought only last week is suddenly dated or obsolete today. Foods and vitamins are "new and improved." Styles change every six months. New car models are heralded yearly. And all of this fluctuation engulfs us on television, on the radio, before a movie begins in a theater, on billboards, in computer popup ads. Each repeated message delivered to us thousands of times a day has but one aim: to make us buy something so we think we have satisfied our desire.

This is a fast-paced time with new inventions appearing rapidly. Material things are pushed at us through the media and advertising campaigns constantly. A great example is technology, which outdates itself every day.

Desire, Imagination, and Visualization

> "Before we set our hearts too much upon anything,
> let us examine how happy they are,
> who already possess it."
> —*Francois de La Rochefoucauld*

But what about a desire for qualities like serenity, peace, love, and beauty?

What about a desire for a sense of confidence and self-worth? Health is another important desire not to be overlooked. Everyone wants to be fit, but when you are healthy, do you appreciate it and do you give thanks for it? Or do you only acknowledge health and well-being when something is wrong or when the doctor delivers news you do not want to hear?

Are you giving thanks for your relationships with family and friends, or are you only upset when you feel lonely?

We tend to forget such blessings and take them for granted, but they are much more important than all the material things anyone can possess. Does the new house matter when you have fallen seriously ill or have gotten injured in an accident? Have you not experienced this perspective? Does such a painful experience not provide clarity?

> **"Whatever you vividly imagine, ardently desire, sincerely believe, and enthusiastically act upon... must inevitably come to pass!"**
> —*Paul J. Meyer*

"...because you can!"

Look at desire from a higher viewpoint

Your desire is a spark in your Consciousness pressing for expression. Life is unfolding itself. Life always presses for manifestation and progress. It is an ever-changing, ongoing process. Like water, life flows.

Intelligence, or what many call God, is the all power and all-knowing substance, the creator of the Universe. You are part of this substance, and you and your environment are constantly recreated through your thoughts and desires and manifested into the visible realm.

Whatever you focus on the most comes to fruition. As soon as you start thinking about something specific, giving it sufficient feeling and having a sincere desire for it, your creative mind goes into action and immediately brings into being the thing wished for. You have become your own genie.

"Be careful what you wish for" is an important warning as thinking and feeling create visible thought conclusions, good or bad. Therefore, wish only for the good, pure, lovely, and the kind and generous so you won't manifest suffering or unpleasant experiences for yourself.

> "Life isn't about finding yourself.
> Life is about creating yourself."
> —*George Bernard Shaw*

How does desire work?

"Desire is ever the father" or first spark; it is the starting point in the creative process. After you have

Desire, Imagination, and Visualization

outlined the desire, you have to reason carefully, determine its purpose, and imagine and visualize the details. You will arrive at a conclusion about the object or occurrence desired. When this feeling or conviction is strong enough and all doubt has vanished, you will experience the outcome or manifestation in the visible world.

Everything you see and experience in your surroundings is a shadow or image of your thoughts and beliefs. You alone can think for yourself and your world. You alone know what your true desires are and what your heart really feels. No one can think for you, and no one sees the world exactly the same way. You are unique and so am I. Not one of us is exactly the same, and not one of us sees the world in the same light. It is all individual, and it is all mental.

You also have to develop unlimited thinking and open your heart to the ideas of perfect health, wealth, and happiness. Unlimited thinking is knowing that all is possible and everything is available to you right here and right now, allowing you to create your wildest and most wonderful dreams.

This will happen if you steadily focus on the outcome of your desires. Let your imagination go beyond the life that you are accustomed to. Step outside your comfort zone. Everything we see—that is, everything that was ever made—was imagined by someone first.

>"All that spirits desire, spirits attain."
>*—Khalid Gibran*

"...because you can!"

Desire at its best with the focus on what you love

Know that it's never too late to start a new venture, finish something you have put on the shelf for a later day, or to restart a forgotten project. Take action on your dreams that have been simmering in your consciousness, and have a clear vision, intent, and plan of execution.

Stay focused and think big. Find creative ways and envision how you will create money, a new home, a better job, more time to yourself, or whatever it is that you desire. Visualize in detail and don't stand in your own way by having doubt and fear about the outcome. Doubt and fear will surely spoil your plan.

Relax. Allow it to happen, and allow yourself to receive the good that is already yours. Acknowledge your power. Grant yourself to enjoy the harvest of the Universe.

Focus only on what you love or find beautiful, and include the sense of awe.

Don't think about what you don't want; think about what you *do* want. It's imperative that you don't waste your energy on anything that's negative or less than good. It will take practice keeping your thoughts in line with what is true and good about your desire, but it's well worth it.

"Only as high as I reach I grow, only as far as I seek can I go, only as deep as I look I can see, only as much as I dream can I be."
—*Karen Ravn*

What will you do with it when you have it? Will you enjoy it?

At the beginning stages of your creation process, if you consider the joy this desire will bring you, you will make better choices. As you know by now, your thoughts are like magnets; they attract a similar frequency and will bring back to you your primary focus. Knowing clearly what you will do with your desire once accomplished, and the ensuing expectations of enjoyment, will prevent you from making costly mistakes.

Make it a habit to think positive always. Impossible, you say? Well, make the effort and improve your thoughts step by step, little by little, like going to a mental gym. Your thought muscles will become stronger and stronger.

> **"What we can or cannot do, what we consider possible or impossible, is rarely a function of our true capability. It is more likely a function of our beliefs about who we are."**
> *—Tony Robbins*

Prepare and clarify your desire

Renew your Soul by spending quiet, reflective time by yourself and really listening to what your inner voice tells you. Remember, you already know the answers. They are already within you.

You are now preparing for the creation of your desire, so you have to be very clear on how you feel about it.

"...because you can!"

Ask yourself the following questions: What do I really desire? Is it travel, a relationship, painting, making music, teaching, nursing, tech stuff? Do I want to change my career but am I too scared? Is this the right desire for me? What will I do with it when I have it? Is it good for everyone involved? Will I really enjoy my desire?

The more questions you ask yourself, and the clearer you are with your ideas, the clearer the outcome will be. Make a list of goals you would like to achieve. Make a list of things you love and cherish but that need your attention. Or make a wish list of unfinished projects that you've put aside. You know that their accomplishments would make you happier.

Here are some more questions to ask yourself: What would improve my daily routine? What is lacking in my world right now? What would make my life feel complete?

> "Once you make a decision, the universe conspires to make it happen."
> —*Ralph Waldo Emerson*

Take action

Now that you have clarified your plan, you can take action by setting the creative thought force in motion.

Be assured that the more you evolve, the more powerful your thoughts will become. Your self-confidence will grow, and your solid, instant convictions will help manifest your desire quicker. During this

Desire, Imagination, and Visualization

process, always expect the best to happen. Never expect failure.

Thought repetition, focus, and attention to detail are important. Your sub-consciousness will store the information and your mental images and immediately start producing your desire. At the point of conviction that "it is so," it will manifest into your visible world. As within (your mentality), so without (visible experience) cannot be said often enough.

You live in a perfect Universe, so take your share. You deserve it. It is your right to have the desire fulfilled of being happy, healthy, and abundantly supplied.

> **"All the works of man have their origin in creative fantasy. What rights do have we then to depreciate imagination?"**
> —*Carl Jung*

Have fun with your imagination

Develop your imagination. See it as a game, and play with it. It takes practice to imagine correctly and, like anything that needs to be learned, it's an art. It gives you the ability to step outside your personal limits, to step outside your box. You can imagine anything you want: play, explore, and have fun with it! So imagine the best for you and everyone as it is the starting point of creation.

As mentioned before, everything you see was imagined by someone first before it could be made manifest in the visible realm of this world. All inventions started in the minds of the inventors. All the buildings and bridges, for example, started in the minds of the architects. All the books in the world began as thoughts. Nothing was made without active thought, desire, and imagination. Think about it!

"All successful people, men and women, are big dreamers. They imagine what their future could be, ideal in every respect, and then they work every day toward their distant vision, that goal or purpose."
—*Brian Tracy*

Imagine that!

A good friend of mine shared this uplifting story about his childhood and the power of thought. The mental Law of "Thinking is Causative" always works, even in a young child's immature mind.

Virgil's Story

"When my brother and I were children, the pediatrician told my parents that my brother would be in the 'average range of height' as an adult, approximately five feet and nine inches. Regarding me, the doctor said I would be on the shorter side of average. This was a rather polite way of saying short. However, this was not a great surprise to my parents. My father was five feet six inches and my mother only five feet three inches. My grandparents were all between five feet one and five feet seven inches. My maternal great-grandfather was the only one that reached six feet tall according to my grandmother.

For years my parents frequently remarked that I would be built like my maternal grandfather, described rather fondly as short and stocky. This remark was invariably reiterated whenever a relative would visit. However, this comparison was quite upsetting to me since most of the stories regarding my grandfather, who had passed when I was an infant, were anything than flattering in my mind.

On the other hand, the stories of my six-foot-tall grandfather were almost heroic in proportion. Since it was unwise to counter the wisdom of adults when I was young, I never verbally refuted their comparisons. In my mind, which was both very active and rather creative, an entirely different response took place. Whenever I would hear the comparison I would smile politely but in my mind would shout 'NO!' and I would picture myself as tall and slim. As the time marched on, I did not worry as my brother, who was two years older than I, began to fulfill the pediatrician's prophecy. He eventually reached the height of five foot nine. Although I remained short and stocky until my junior year in high school, I was absolutely convinced I would be tall and continued to mentally picture myself as growing taller and taller, which in my imagination was just over six feet in height.

A great deal of time has passed since I was a 'short and stocky' little lad. I reached my full height

"...because you can!"

of six feet and one quarter inch at the age of twenty-one. Within my generation I was the tallest of my siblings and cousins. Moving on to the next generation, my nieces and nephews all still only range from five feet three to five feet nine...genetics or the power of mind, you decide!"

**"Imagination has brought mankind through the dark ages to its present state of civilization. Imagination led Columbus to discover America. Imagination led Franklin to discover electricity."
—L. Frank Baum**

The ingredients of Visualization and Imagination

We *are* creative mind; we *are* imagination. Any time a thought arises, we imagine what is, could be, would have been, or was. Our imagination is endless, and we should use it constructively. We can visualize in detail that what we want to accomplish, and thereby intensify the desire. Visualization will make your desire more realistic; it will become tangible.

The instruments that we work with daily are thoughts and ideas, colored by imagination. Knowingly or not we create constantly by forming a mental picture in our mind, accepting it for real and then manifesting it out into the visible world.

We are reflecting our creation back to us like a mirror. Thankfully we do not manifest fleeting thoughts; we only express what we perceive as possible or real.

Desire, Imagination, and Visualization

To clarify how consciousness works, it must be pointed out that we have one consciousness with twofold states. One is our conscious consciousness, which controls our daily thoughts and activities. The other is the subconscious, the sum total that stores our past experiences, beliefs, inherent tendencies, taught information, accumulated mass consciousness, and mass beliefs. It is still *one* (consciousness) with two functions.

Psychologists regard the subconscious as the "pushed back" accumulated ideas of your life. It contains your life experiences starting from birth. One could argue that it started before birth but, since the subject has not been proven, it will not be discussed here. You will have to deal with both the subconscious and consciousness in order to gain the proper understanding.

"Inspiration is God making contact with itself."
—*Ram Dass*

Awaken your imagination

Play with your creative thoughts and envision the best possible life. Like many talents, imagination is dormant in so many people. Their vision is short and predictable, and they do not dare to envision more for themselves. You deserve to dream; it is an important part of your road to a better life.

When you have a desire that you are actively working on, you will find excitement and enthusiasm reappear and reenter your mind. You will feel love and compassion for your project; you will be tireless and exuberant.

Love, love, love what you do, and it will come to pass. Our outer world reflects the imagination held in our mind. We are what we imagine ourselves to be.

Every person must become conscious of this fact. Everyone has to find out for him- or herself. What a comfort it is to know that my experiences are the result of my own beliefs. It is a blessing to know that no one can hurt or affect me or my experiences.

"Life is a pilgrimage. The wise man does not rest by the roadside inns. He marches direct to the illimitable domain of eternal bliss, his ultimate destination."
—*Swami Sivananda*

It is necessary to have aim in life

Without aim in life, we drift and wander. We must have focus and determination; we must know what we want. Expectancy and desire must become one.

A good exercise is to create a vision board. Lay out the ideal picture of your desires by finding photos or clippings from magazines that speak to you either in color, content, or image. Arrange them in a collage using a piece of cardboard, and make it your vision on a board.

A visual stimulant, the vision board will help you to focus on what your ideal world would look like. It's quite fun. You might be surprised!

"Visualization is daydreaming with a purpose."
—*Bo Bennett*

Right inner speech

Another practical exercise is to listen to your inner speech. If you pay attention, you will notice that we talk to ourselves all the time. This observation will reveal to you what you really think and feel about yourself and how you view the world. Your word habits project your true self.

Start a new, positive, and constructive inner speech to match the outside picture you want to experience. Correct (i.e., positive) inner speech is essential, so listen to the words you use. Words and the way we use them are our most valuable tool. Realize that words have meanings, and you have to get in the habit of omitting words and phrases such as "I *hate* such and such" or "I'd *die* to see this or that." Words to avoid include the following: despise, evil, ugly, horror, rotten, sick, trouble, and so forth.

Keep a log of the negative words you use, and then find better words to replace this harmful, pessimistic verbiage. For example, instead of "this is ugly," you might use "this is unpleasant to look at." Instead of "I hate this dress," you can say "I dislike this dress." "I'd die to see that movie" should instead be "I'm excited to see that movie," and so on.

After you've improved your word patterns, inside and out, you can take it to an even higher level. Once

"...because you can!"

negativity is eliminated, you'll learn to truly speak the language of love. Using words correctly will build you up and empower you. It's part of the package.

"Love of beauty is taste. The creation of beauty is art."
—*Ralph Waldo Emerson*

Discovering what you want

What would it mean to you if you said, "I want to live in a better apartment"? For any desire, you must discover the essence or purpose of that desire. What will you have gained? Will a better apartment satisfy you, make you happy, and fulfill you? Or will it leave you wanting more?

Let's say you are thinking of buying a house. Does a house mean security, status, comfort, or a place to call home? What does a place called home mean to you? Keep asking yourself questions and answer them honestly. This is the way to "know thyself."

In your desires you will find patterns that reveal your likes and dislikes. You will discover a common thread in your answers, which will show you what you really want. You will find your true self and, through this awareness, you will create beautiful things. You will create *right* things for you.

It is necessary to stay open-minded in the creation process. Do not be rigid and stubborn by limiting yourself to a specific way of "wanting it to be." As you find out what you want in detail, allow the all-knowing

Desire, Imagination, and Visualization

Universe to speak to you and guide you. Stay fluid and flexible, not wavering or indecisive; be bendable enough to hear the inner voice guide you.

The same principle should be applied to money. If it is money that you want or need, know beforehand how you will use it. You don't need money just to have it. Focus instead on the thing you want rather than the money itself.

What you want, if it's a material thing, doesn't have to be paid necessarily with money. Abundance comes from a number of different sources and through many channels. Remember, it's the spiritual coin, that sense of abundance that fulfills your needs.

More on this subject will be discussed in the Abundance chapter.

"You cannot escape the results of your thoughts. Whatever your present environment may be, you will fall, remain or rise with your thoughts, your vision, your ideal. You will become as small as your controlling desire; as great as your dominant aspiration."
—*James Lane Allen*

Last but not least

Any desire has an essence or purpose, so know the essence or purpose of what you want. The essence of a car would be that you want better and more reliable transportation, getting you from one place to another. The essence of this book is to help others to live a more harmonious life.

"...because you can!"

When you visualize your desire, picturing the purpose or goal is vital. The most important detail, however, is to put *yourself* in the picture.

The more vividly you can picture the scene or item you want, with you included, the better. See the images in vivid bright colors, mentally feel the textures and smells associated, and bring in the sense of good quality. This intense visual makes the images more real to you. It has to become real in your mind before it can manifest as a real object in this world.

As an example, in my case, I fully expect to publish this book and start inspirational workshops. My approach to this project is as follows:

I can see the book cover, feel the pages, and see my photo on the back of the book jacket. I have done research and have talked to publishers. I have pictured myself in detail at book signings and seminars. I have been busy focusing on writing these pages.

I have magnetized and attracted people that want to be part of this project. I envision a team that is honest, sincere, creative, enthusiastic, and equally interested in the success of this venture, as it will benefit everyone involved, including myself.

My daily mantra is this: "The essence of what I want is a successful business that serves others by improving their life experience. I fully expect to be in the right place at the right time. This desire will unfold naturally without effort or strain. It will bring me joy and happiness."

> **"Do not dwell in the past, do not dream of the future, concentrate the mind on the present moment."**
> *—Buddha*

How can our desires benefit others?

Let us also include the welfare of all people on our wish list of desires. Let them be part of our new ventures. Let us embrace everyone in this wonderful life we are creating. Let us be willing to give freely as we will receive in exact proportion. Let us wish happiness and success for those with whom we come into contact. Let us contribute and serve, help and support others in their life's journey.

Freely sharing part of "us" and our talents with the world is part of the mission to contribute to Universal Harmony.

Ask yourself, How can I serve and contribute my talents to the world? How can I make a difference?

I'm not saying march in demonstrations or stand in a picket line or protest a war. I'm saying make a difference by being helpful, kind, generous, and patient. Give of your talent and time. Start building your inner peace.

Imagine, visualize, and dream; dream as big as you can. Create your heaven here on earth…because you can!

ANSWER THESE QUESTIONS HONESTLY:

1. What are your true desires?
2. Are your desires in conformity with your soul or just wishes for material riches?
3. What do you think will make you fulfilled?
4. What will make you a better person?
5. What is lacking in your world right now? What would make your life complete?
6. What will you do when you accomplish your desire? How will it make you feel?
7. Are you flexible enough to go with your inner voice?
8. How do you fulfill the desire of abundance?
9. How can your desire benefit others? Are you including others in your life's picture?
10. How can you make a difference, even in one person's life?

CHAPTER 5

YOU ARE IMPORTANT

As pointed out in the previous chapters, this is all about you.

> **"The only journey is the one within."**
> *—Rainer Maria Rilke*

What, who, and where are you? Wouldn't you like to know?

"You" is all there is in your world just as "I" am all there is in my world. There is nothing else for you but your sense of self, and there is nothing else for me but my sense of self.

Let us make the best of our lives here on Earth. Let us be part of the Universal dance and the creation process. Let us be aware of the good we can do and want to do for ourselves, humankind, the planet, and all of its creatures.

You, the only creator in your life experience, are a mental being, not a mere physical human. You are the Soul, the unlimited potential; you are part of and connected to the Source of all Being.

You are not a small insignificant person, struggling every day to make a living or to just get by. It feels like that sometimes only because you do not know who and what you really are.

You are not the body that you inhabit; it is only a vessel you use, your identity on this plane of being. You are a Soul that animates this body, proven by what we call death, a time when the Soul departs and leaves the physical presence behind. The life that appears to be in the body belongs to the Soul.

"You don't have a soul. You are a Soul. You have a body."
—*C. S. Lewis*

Life is cause—body only effect. Your body never had life of its own to begin with.

It is a manifestation, a shadow of your beliefs and convictions suitable for this plane. It is a symbol of identification, necessary to "fit in" here and now. But the true *you* is your Soul, your Spirit, your Consciousness. It is part of the Universal, all-powerful essence called God.

Knowing who and what God consists of, as we discussed in the first chapter, is the key. By reading this book and contemplating its essence, you will learn about *all* that you are. You will be challenged to practice and apply this knowledge.

Where are you? You are right here right now. You are in your awareness of yourself; you are in your recognition of the "I AM." In other words, you are where your thought is at any given moment.

For example, I can be at a place called Los Angeles in my office, but my thoughts are back east, thinking of my son's upcoming wedding. Concentrating on the details of wedding preparations, my physical surroundings at this moment fade away. In my mind are vivid pictures of the happenings in a far away location. Thus, I am engaged in my imagination. I feel like I'm there because I am transported to another "place" in mind. Although I have not moved, I have traveled mentally because all I can ever be is in my mind, my imagination, and my sense of self.

I am where my mind is, my mind is where I am, and my thoughts are always now.

> **"The man who never in his mind and thoughts traveled to heaven is no artist."**
> **—*William Blake***

You are Cause with a corresponding Effect

It should be obvious to any thinker that if we understand cause, we can control the effect. As we learn that we (our Spirit's activity, which is our thinking) are causative, we are also discovering that we are responsible for the effects we experience.

As we understand the cause responsible for those manifestations, we ultimately will be able to control our body and life experiences harmoniously and at will.

With this understanding, we can consciously create only that which is good and desirable—namely, health and happiness. The same is true of the effect known as wealth. However, you have to learn that your mind causes these events, and how and why it causes them.

Additionally, the importance of love and good feeling in this work cannot be over-stressed. It is the vital element in your life's journey. Without love, nothing will satisfy or fulfill you in your quest.

A sincere want for goodness and interest in life, in general, is crucial.

Be frank with yourself and realize that you have to do the work and set aside a certain portion of each day for reading and thinking. Thinking about how life works and how to improve *your part* of this life is the essence of your daily mental duties.

Don't take the unfoldment of your life lightly or be careless in your choices.

Take advantage of the many books available today and the unlimited sources of wisdom in this Internet age. "Seek and ye shall find." An experienced teacher or guide can show you the way, but you must do the traveling.

No excuses. Don't say you don't have time. Make time! What can possibly be more important than learning how to achieve a more fulfilling and more harmonious life?

"Love is from the infinite, and will remain until eternity. The seeker of love escapes the chains of birth and death. Tomorrow, when resurrection comes, the heart that is not in love will fail the test."
—*Rumi*

Forever and ever?

This is an ongoing process, so the unfoldment of your Understanding will never be finished. There will never, in fact, come a time that we understand all there is to know. Mind/consciousness is unlimited, and there will always be more to grasp and unfold. Though it is hard to comprehend, it is also a wonderful, exciting insight that gives you substance for thought forever and ever.

Do not mistake that which you see as Life itself. Life cannot be seen with the mortal eye other than by the reflection it produces. Compare it to the wind. You cannot see the wind unless you look at the movement of the trees and the soft swaying of the grasses and all of Nature itself.

"...because you can!"

What you see is only effect. It is your perception—or your sense of—what you see or what it means to you. You are this life; you are part of all that you see, hear, touch, smell, and you are the cause of all that befalls you every day of your life!

> **"Life finds its purpose and fulfillment in the expansion of happiness."**
> **—*Maharishi Mahesh Yogi***

Your purpose

Your purpose is "to be happy and to joyfully participate in the creativity and evolution of the Universe" (Wayne Dyer). Clearly, your purpose is "to unfold yourself and through conscious recognition enjoy the fullness and goodness" (William W. Walter). You are here to learn your life's lessons and to enjoy the process.

You are a living cause and are constantly causing, and through the conscious awareness of the good you are causing, you will find yourself enjoying your creations. You have free will and can choose anything you want.

I know some of you will come up with all kinds of excuses—why you can't do what you should do, or want to do.

Stop!

Look at your situation and develop a solution that will work, a solution that will bring you closer to happiness. Any situation can be improved, and all your negative experiences will disappear if you stop acknowledging those negative conditions. For many people, the *drama* of the negative holds their attention too often because it feels exciting at the moment. But drama is always negative energy.

People might be bored with their daily routines and want more excitement. Subconsciously, they think they need the drama to feel emotion. Emotion is a strong sensation, like a drug. Many men and women use negative emotions to feel alive.

We all know how stories are repeatedly shown on TV about violent acts or catastrophes or scandals. Such negativity offers a false sense of escape. The tragedies of others distract us from seeking introspection about our own lives. The woes of others make us feel better about our own problems. We are fascinated with this false image because it aids in the avoidance of our own issues.

Stop again!

It's all wasted energy. Yes, we are drawn into situations and circumstances for different reasons, but they are always self-inflicted.

Subconsciously, we are acting out what we have learned or accepted from our past as true. Our subconscious is a storehouse of our beliefs, impressions, assumptions, judgments, and feelings based on past experiences and even unfulfilled dreams and desires.

"...because you can!"

So we have explosive emotions at our fingertips, just waiting to come to the surface.

The slightest thought sets mind vibration in motion. The mind is a magnet, so it will attract what you wish for. However, we attract what we think most of. We attract what we feel is real. Thankfully, we do not manifest every thought, as most of them are not strong enough to be expressed into the visible.

Think of the consequences if we acted out every thought that crossed our minds!

Wouldn't that be something?

So the fact is, we are an image-making machine. You are an image maker.

On a mental level, pure consciousness cannot be destroyed; it can only be expressed and multiplied. Because it is a circulating center in Infinity, nothing in the Universe can ever be lost. There is always more, there is always enough, and it is always unlimited.

The purpose of the Universe is the same as your purpose. It is to find self-expression, amazingly enough through you!

"There are no extra pieces in the Universe. Everyone is here because he or she has a place to fill, and every piece must fit itself into the big jigsaw puzzle."
—Deepak Chopra

Believe in yourself and do what you want

The "Secret" is not a secret. Causative thought is the natural workings of the Universe. It is and always has been; there is nothing mysterious about it.

Consider feelings you may have about the work you do for a living. Work, when looked at as hard labor or strenuous effort, becomes unsatisfying and unfulfilling. If you look at it as strenuous, tedious, uneventful, and unfulfilling, your job becomes nothing more than a burden, something that you have to get up to and slog through each day, a detriment to enjoying life and discovering balance and happiness.

It is a chore, something you feel you have to do to earn a living, something that is dreadful and a burden. This is no way to spend your life.

But when you are working on a project or endeavor, and it is your heart's desire, work becomes play. Hours spent focused on what you love is not labor. You need to examine your work and make the necessary adjustments if it is not providing any level of satisfaction.

If you don't see a way out of your current situation at this time, at least make the best out of it.

"The greatest glory in living lies not in never falling, but in rising every time we fall."
—Ralph Waldo Emerson

If you are ready to improve your work environment, let's use your place of employment as an example.

"...because you can!"

Let's change your attitude and lift your pessimistic outlook.

First, look at your choice of employment through the eyes of love. Second, find good things about your job and write them down. Maybe you really like your boss, or your co-workers are your friends. Maybe the job is located close to home and convenient to get to. Maybe it provides benefits like healthcare, a pension plan, or other financial bonuses.

Do you find joy in your daily work?

Find all the good reasons why your job is really great, and stop saying, "Yes, but..." You will see your job environment change as your sense regarding work changes. Believe it or not, you created your job for you, so do the best you can.

If it seems that your job is hopeless and you are longing for a new vocation or creative outlet, remember life's celebrations can be found elsewhere, outside the work environment—for example, those treasures like backyard get-togethers, quiet walks, teaching yourself how to play a musical instrument, auditioning for a local play, joining a hiking club, volunteering, and so on.

The networking that comes with mingling with other people under a variety of circumstances often leads to vocational opportunities never previously considered.

Appreciate what you have now in *all* areas of your life so you can multiply this good and create even more of what you desire.

Opportunity will knock, so listen and let it in. Many times we miss opportunities by being too busy or ignoring our inner voice. We do not listen to our instincts.

Don't block your senses with discouragement, negativity, and doubt. Let the door remain wide open to love, success, and new adventures—maybe even a new path. You are meant to have the best. Life is an opportunity to grow and learn something new every moment.

"Trust that little voice in your head that says 'Wouldn't it be interesting if...', And then do it."
—*Duane Michals*

New Year's resolutions

Many people set goals at the beginning of the New Year, but shortly after their commitment to better themselves, they give up.

I have made a goal list every year for over twenty years. It's interesting to note the progress I've made, but also what continues in my life. My list shows a pattern of desires; it also shows growth and change. I look and reflect on it often and adjust my focus as necessary. I keep the journal fluid and flexible, but I stay on track and accomplish about 90 percent of the yearly quota.

Try making your own goal list that supports your focus. Think it through and be specific with the items on your list. Work on achieving your goals step by step. You have to start somewhere.

"...because you can!"

Personal goals might include working on your relationship or buying a new home. You career goals might include a promotion or your renewed commitment to a more efficient business plan. Spiritual goals might include taking more time for yourself and reading inspirational books. Your achievement of these goals will result in Happiness.

Even your smallest desire should be on your goal list because each is a stepping stone toward harmony and happiness and fulfillment. Checking off each item after you've met your goal will give you a sense of accomplishment and confidence. You will then move forward and bring about larger goals and dreams. It is all a process.

Remember the Universe is organized and systematized, and so are you. It just takes a little practice!

"There are only two mistakes one can make along the road to truth; not going all the way, and not starting."
—Buddha

Helpful points

- **Believe in yourself**
    Believing in yourself, your specific mind-set, your determination, and your patterns and habits in life will determine your success in everything you do.

- **Everything is within reach**
    Realize what you imagine as true. When you visualize your desire, it already exists in another

dimension of mind. Everything is within reach; you only have to bring it into this state of mind.

- **Be flexible**

    When during your journey you encounter resistance, and it's just not working out easily, don't try to force it. There is always a good reason why it's not moving in your direction. Remember the Universe knows all and knows what is good for you.

- **Listen**

    Be still and listen carefully to your inner voice. The right thoughts will come to you during your quiet moments of contemplation, so act courageously on your instincts.

- **Be patient**

    Flow with it. Universal intelligence knows all and will guide you if you just let it; it knows the proper time. It does not hurry.

- **Show determination**

    Don't give up easily. When you first start working on the changes, you're thinking and feeling, and your circumstances don't always improve immediately. Just remember that you have been thinking incorrectly and have been misdirected for so long. It takes at least 51 percent of right thought to tip the scale and get you right results.

- **Stick with it**

    Talk about what you love, about your desires, and hear yourself speak. Observe yourself feel and get excited, and take joy in the sensation you derive when you sense you are functioning as part of the Universe. With the knowledge of how creation works and your vivid imagination, the image desired will harden into fact.

Talk about what's good today, and omit all talk or gossip to the contrary. Catch yourself when you want to chime in, and stop yourself. Don't be a part of the negative propaganda you hear and see everywhere. Stick to your concept and desire. Do not waver or doubt.

- **Feel it**
  All of your endeavors should have an accompanying good feeling of love, confidence, and appreciation. Especially your love for yourself and what you have created is imperative.

In my daily workings, I constantly think and feel that "I have such a great life." I really, really feel it. I repeat it daily, and looking around me and listening to the voice deep inside of me, I can truly say, "I have such a great life."

And even when events in my life are sometimes pressing and challenging, I will see them for what they are and move on to a more positive frame of mind because they are nothing more than a test of my understanding, helping me to learn and grow.

A deep appreciation and a tremendous sense of gratefulness spring from this awareness, and it overcomes and floods my whole being; my soul is filled with love for life.

I challenge you to try it! The rewards are wonderful. Test it. Give it a chance!

> **"All that we are is the result of what we have thought. If a man speaks or acts with an evil thought, pain follows him. If a man speaks or acts with a pure thought, happiness follows him, like a shadow that never leaves him."**
> **—Buddha**

Again, it's all about YOU

Throughout this book, I will continue to ask you many questions, so I want you to think, reason, and question yourself. It is important to know who you are and what you want out of life.

You essentially live in your own head (your mind). Thoughts, impressions, judgments, and reactions impact everything you will do. You are busy in your own head. What is created in your mind is the starting point of all you do, and you can change it if it needs changing.

Many people just drift and try to get through the day with as little effort as possible. Many of them are so busy running around all day that they think they just don't have the time or energy for self-improvement.

A friend once told me after reading one of my articles, "You bring up a lot of good questions and ideas that, I have to admit, are beyond my ability (or desire) for self-reflection. So many feelings to process, that I'm kind of glossing them over so I can just function." Needless to say, his life is chaotic and out of balance.

Sadly enough, when people close their minds, no one can help or be of guidance. But as we are individuals and on the same path, sooner or later they will find what is necessary to show them the way. As we all know, "You can lead the horse to the water, but you cannot make it drink."

"All the breaks you need in life wait within your imagination; Imagination is the workshop of your mind, capable of turning mind energy into accomplishment and wealth."
—*Napoleon Hill*

People. Are they part of you?

When looking at life properly, it is magical and fascinating. Life is Love. Love is transforming. Love is a motivator; it makes you do things. So if you don't want to do something, start loving it and it will become a joy.

It is the same situation for people. People are a reflection of you and your sense of them. People can be wonderful and fun, but they can also be irritating and annoying. It is your sense and perspective that has to change.

As your sense changes, the world and its inhabitants around you change accordingly.

Often as our perspective changes, so do reactions from people who were our friends. For one reason or another, a certain friend does not call you anymore. For you, it might be a really dramatic experience as you have no idea what happened and why. People you've known for a long time are too busy to check in with you. Co-workers have other lunch plans, and you find yourself asking why.

Assuming you are still your lovely self, nothing has happened. You merely lifted your sense of life and shifted to another frequency. In no time, other doors will open and new people will enter your life's experience, people that are on the same frequency. Isn't it great?

"I want you to be concerned about your next door neighbor. Do you know your next door neighbor?"
—Mother Teresa

To give you an example of how it works, look at certain groups of people like charitable entities supporting a certain cause: health club members, artists and musicians, literary folks, religious groups, and even protesters and sports fanatics, to name a few. (This goes as far as people who are only interested in physical beauty or people that see violence as part of their lives such as gangs. And the list goes on and on.)

The old saying "Birds of a feather, flock together" is also true in the mental realm.

Like-minded people always find each other, and you will attract individuals with similar values, goals, mind-sets, and capacity to love. Your friends will either change or grow with you over time. Yes, they may move on. "I've outgrown him or her." Haven't you heard someone say that or felt it about folks who for years were your friends?

I have a friend of thirty years who has changed with me in spiritual matters; even so, we have our own separate lives. Over the years, we have managed to stay on the same frequency. However, most of the people I've known during my lifetime have changed or have gone their own way.

Think back in your life and really see the flow of people ever changing and fitting into your world, at any given time. Even the unlovely and unkind had their place. You needed them and you created them so you could learn something. It might have been a painful lesson at the time, but you gained from it. Hopefully, you are better for it now. The ones on your frequency have most likely stayed with you.

"The greatest wisdom is seeing through appearances."
—*Atisha*

You are learning to use the power within

You are at the point of stopping to look outside yourself and are ready to take responsibility for your actions. You no longer require help from someone else, and you are able to deal with your own affairs from a new viewpoint. You are ready to look within.

You Are Important

The moment you realize that you can use the creative power of your thought, you will be free. You will start anew.

Christians refer to this as being "reborn." Muslims have the saying "die before you die," and my neighbor's friend puts it like this: "Shedding dead skin like a snake." In the Bible, in 1 Corinthians 15:31, Paul states, "I die daily." No matter what the expression, it all means the same.

We have to let go of the old beliefs, transform, and start fresh with this newfound wisdom. And we have to do this daily.

Only ignorance can hold you back. Only fear can stifle you. Get busy causing and creating for yourself the good things you have always wanted.

Don't be afraid when something unforeseen happens. Trust me, deep down we always know what is in store for us and when it's coming. Our mortal minds are just not in tune with our spiritual selves, and we block out the light of mind. Accept it and embrace it; muster up all your courage and know the future will be even better than you've dreamed.

"Death is a stripping away of all that is not you. The secret of life is to 'die before you die'—and find that there is no death."
—Eckhart Tolle

Change

As I am entering a new phase in life, many "things" have "gone" away. It seems that part of the life I once knew has faded away like the summer mist, while some things that I enjoy have continued. This process is ongoing and it will continue to be: to change, to fade, to reoccur, and to evolve. It is this way with everyone, including you.

So what has changed?

Nothing really! I have only changed my sense of self, my sense of who I am and who I want to be and, therefore, I have been given the opportunity of change.

In my case, I have asked for and received the gift of time. I am now able to focus on my purpose of teaching and writing in solitude. I am given the possibility to expand, and I am expressing growth.

It will evolve and change again because this is the way of the Universe. And I will adapt...because I can!

"The conscious mind may be compared to a fountain playing in the sun and falling back into the great subterranean pool of subconscious from which it rises."
—*Sigmund Freud*

ANSWER THESE QUESTIONS HONESTLY:

1. What are you?
2. Who are you?
3. Where are you?
4. What is your purpose?
5. Will you take time to study, read, and work on your unfoldment?
6. How does your thought create? Be specific.
7. Do you find joy in your work and, if not, how can you improve this situation?
8. List five people on your current frequency and five that have "left" your realm.
9. What is your best sense of "to be reborn"? What does it mean to you?
10. Start a journal and document your daily evolvement.

CHAPTER 6

THOUGHT AND ITS CORRECT APPLICATION

Why do you think the thoughts you think?

How come one day you are happy and one day you are sad? Why are you hopeful and excited today and in despair tomorrow?

Do you think about these things? Do you look at your moods and thought habits? Do you consider them good or bad? Do you want to change and improve yourself, or do you want to stay the same because you think you are doing just fine?

"Taking the first step with the good thought, the second with the good word, and the third with the good deed, I enter paradise."
—*Persian proverb*

Could you do better?

I think we can agree that we all could reach for better. "Being good" is always relative to what you think "good" is, or what your current perception of good entails. Couldn't we all be less judgmental, kinder, more patient, more tolerant, more giving, more loving, and so on?

"We are what we think. All that we are arises with our thoughts. With our thoughts, we make the world."
—Buddha

My intent, in writing this book, is to ask you many questions about yourself in order for you to get to know yourself. Step back and examine yourself. I believe that you can find the answers to your questions through diligent study of the Laws of mind and by your strong desire to know how life truly works.

I am naturally a curious person. I ask myself questions all the time, and I always want to know why it works the way it works; so the questions come easily and so do the answers.

A mentor's spiritual guidance will provide significant help along the way and will spark ideas that may be dormant in your mind. Explore your innermost thoughts and feelings by thinking of it as a treasure hunt. If you approach the process calmly, the reward of self-discovery will be exuberant. It will literally open your eyes.

Thought and Its Correct Application

> **"No one can see their reflection in running water. It is only in still water that we can see."**
> —*Taoist proverb*

You must "want to know." You need to "want to correct yourself" and "want to improve your negative thought habits."

Self-correction is not a dreadful task; it should be a joyful and uplifting undertaking, with a sincere desire to be right—not right in opinion but right according to Universal Law.

Make the commitment that you will cherish yourself. You will set aside quiet time, love yourself, and listen to yourself. Start treating yourself kindly and respectfully. Let go of guilt, shame, poor self-esteem, and all thoughts lesser than those that are pure, good, and lovely.

> **"Live your life as though your every act were to become a universal law."**
> —*Immanuel Kant*

Don't correct yourself tomorrow; correct yourself NOW

Utilize what you know, even if you're at a starting point, and give recognition to your accomplishments to date. Praise yourself for the good work you have done.

"...because you can!"

Harmony is natural; discord is unnatural. And gratitude is one of the greatest healers. So trust your source; trust your instincts and listen carefully.

Practice making each thought being better than the one before. Keeping a diary with daily notes will help you to see a pattern. Observe your behavior and word habits. We don't always realize the power of the words we frequently use. In fact, too often we use them without thinking.

There exists an unfortunate amount of negativity in our language—phrases and expressions and simple words reflecting our careless speech. Often, when a situation arises, we revert to the negative: "Oh God, what happened now?" or "Why me again?" or "It's always the same problem!" These are just a few of the phrases that express the expectancy of wrong or evil.

For fun, make a list of the negative phrases and reactions you use or hear daily.

My neighbor made a wonderful comment the other day. He was a little overwhelmed with the extent of his kitchen remodel and said, "Well, I can look at this in two different ways. I can say, 'Oh man, what a mess! I can't wait to get this over with.' Or I can say, 'WOW, I am getting a new, beautiful kitchen.' What the heck am I complaining about? How lucky am I!"

This is exactly what I want you to practice. Take any negative viewpoint and turn it around. You are the luckiest person you know, no matter what the situation. You are fortunate and blessed because you are alive, you are in charge of your life, you are intelligent, and you are a loving being. You are the most precious person you know.

"People in the West are always getting ready to live."
—Chinese proverb

The right state of mind is ease

Your life should be easy and pleasant, calm, and full of joy. Prove it to yourself by applying the positive exercises shown, celebrating your accomplishments and enjoying life's blessings, no matter how small.

Stop being too busy for the right things in life!

As you learn how to apply right thought and notice progress in your daily life, you will gain the self-confidence needed to achieve even greater goals. Persistence and the ability "to stick with it" are of great importance. Never give up no matter how daunting the circumstances appear to be.

Much has been written about the power of thought, but my intent is to keep matters very practical. It does not help you to know esoteric words and to quote spiritual paradigms if they have no application.

Only practical application of your Understanding will help you to better yourself and improve your daily living. This world is a practical place. "Talking" doesn't help you, but "doing" does.

"...because you can!"

"What matters is to live in the present, live now, for every moment is now. It is your thoughts and acts of the moment that create your future. The outline of your future path already exists, for you created its pattern by your past."
—Sai Baba

What you think right NOW is important

All we have is the present. The past and the future are not important. How you think NOW is important. The future is shaped by your "now" thoughts, as the now was shaped by your past thoughts, beliefs, and convictions. Think right thoughts now, and act in accordance with those right thoughts: feel them, believe them, and your future will be glorious. Changing your thinking will result in good and also abundant experiences.

Know that your past was your immature, dated thinking. So think mature thoughts going forward. Tell yourself "I know I can" because the truth is "you can," so claim all the good there is for yourself and others.

The problems you experience right now are just a "lesser sense" of your concept of yourself. These problems are presented to you only as an opportunity to learn and to teach you a better way of handling daily occurrences.

Through this exercise you will arrive at a more complete understanding of yourself and be capable of correcting your mistakes. Just keep it in the present, stay in the moment, and remember it will always be NOW.

Fresh choices are available every day, at every moment of your existence. You can only think NOW!

"Realize deeply that the present moment is all you have. Make the NOW the primary focus of your life."
—Eckhart Tolle

Imbue feeling in your thoughts

Always put right feeling into your thoughts. Feeling is the key to expressing your desires and manifesting them into the visible. Love your decisions and your conclusions. Feel good about your choices. Love and good feelings will contribute to manifest your desires quicker.

You do not have to acquire any special powers. There is no mysterious secret involved, and it is the natural working of the Law. You don't have to "make" anything because the Universe works the way it works; no one can stop or alter it.

It is Universal Law to always express your thought conclusions. So use it and work with it—not against it!

You already have what it takes within you; you have only to tap into this inert power. Your mind and its activity, which is your thought and your feelings, are the most powerful tools you have. They are always available to you.

> **"The human mind will not be confined to any limits."**
> *—Johann Wolfgang von Goethe*

Your thought consists of your ability to reason and feel

Your thought reasons and feels simultaneously. They are two separate actions, yet one. Reason (the male element in mind) and Feeling (the female element in mind) need to be aligned when demonstrating any manifestation. There is no manifestation if there is no certainty or feeling. You can reason all you want, but unless you arrive at a conclusion, which is a feeling of certainty, nothing will be accomplished.

Even if you experience failure, you held the doubt or the fear of being unsuccessful. Those are strong feelings and, since the Law works the way it works, it will manifest either the good or the bad. Consciousness and its Laws do not know the difference. They only produce.

So in any case, reason leads the way, but when you have reasoned and you have reached a conclusion about your problem, an automatic accompanying feeling will decide the visible outcome.

That is why the right feeling or feeling of Love is so important. No right feeling means no right result. So before you come to a final conclusion, always listen carefully to your heart. Don't rush it; just listen...because your heart knows how you really feel.

You can choose what you think

"Be miserable. Or motivate yourself. Whatever has to be done, it's always your choice."
—Wayne Dyer

Choice is your prerogative, but you must choose happiness, health, and abundance if you want to live a better life. All of these are states of mind. They are not outside of you. They are caused by your thoughts and dispositions, and only you can correct anything that looks less than perfect and good. It sounds simple and it is because you can choose, and you are in charge of your life. This cannot be stated often enough.

You make choices every waking moment, as you chose to read this book right now. You can choose to be happy, to be prosperous and, yes, also to be healthy. Health is certainly a state of mind as we will discuss in the Well-being chapter.

"Every mind must make its choice between truth and repose. It cannot have both."
—Ralph Waldo Emerson

Outline your thoughts

Believe in yourself and your dreams will come true. Outlining your desires and visualizing are two creative ways of planning your future. Be as detailed as you can, and envision your desire as already done. It is finished—already yours. Maintain focus on this outlined picture in your mind, but do not be too stringent and

"...because you can!"

inflexible. The Universe knows best and sometimes will push you in a new direction, showing you a better way.

Soon after I met my husband, we wanted to buy a house. Being on a very limited budget at the time and supporting two small children, we started to look in the area where the apartment we rented was located. We thought the neighborhood was lovely and just right for us. It was, however, in one of the better Los Angeles areas, Hancock Park adjacent, and seemingly out of reach for us.

I had dreamt of having a pool and large backyard. The house could be small, but the outdoors was important to me. We didn't mind hard work and fixing it up.

I pictured it in my mind, visualizing every detail. I was determined to find the right house in the right location, and I would make it work somehow. I could feel it and taste it and I really, really wanted it. After looking around for a couple of weeks and mentally working on my desire, a "For Sale" sign went up half a block down the street from where we lived. It looked like a lovely, smaller fixer upper. When I peeked into the back, I saw a huge backyard with a pool and a beautiful tree.

We called the realtor and it happened to be a divorce situation that warranted a much lower price than market value. The owners were highly motivated to sell. What's more, they had taken it off the market a few months earlier for unknown reasons and then put it back on the listing the exact week that I was looking for our new home.

Thought and Its Correct Application

Everything fell into place, and I knew it was meant to be. We closed escrow in thirty days with very little money down, exactly as much as we could afford. We still, to this day, love our home and have made it into our haven over the years.

When you want something, give it your full attention. Don't entertain doubt, and don't waver in your convictions. You have to believe in yourself, trust in the power of your thought, and visualize and outline your desires with as much feeling as you can muster up. Be patient!

"Our destiny changes with our thought; we shall become what we wish to become, do what we wish to do, when our habitual thought corresponds with our desire."
—*Orison Swett Marden*

What if you think wrong thoughts?

Don't beat yourself up when you make a mistake. Self-condemnation is destructive. You are the all power, perfect, and good, and your mistakes are only your temporary lesser sense of yourself. None of us has unfolded all there is. Making mistakes is part of the natural process and progress.

Simply forgive yourself, and start again.

Each day is a new day. Thankfully, we can correct each thought as it comes, and as soon as we catch the mistaken thought or idea, we can stop being afraid, worrying, and fretting.

"...because you can!"

When you find yourself thinking a lesser thought, go immediately to the opposite, to the right idea. Don't focus on getting rid of something you don't want anymore or on some character trait you need to improve. Instead focus on what you want. If you take your attention away from what you don't want, it will automatically disappear. When you focus on what you do want, it will certainly manifest.

Ensure there are no leftover, old habits and negative thoughts in your subconscious, or they will reappear at any given moment for you to re-examine, solve, and correct. You can be certain that if you let go of your sense of the outgrown habit or negativity, it will disappear. The theory is out of sight, out of mind—or, out of cause, out of effect.

Do not judge by appearances. What you see in this world is only a movie, a mirage, a dream. You are the source of your life experiences. So again, let go of the things you don't want. Life always moves forward. You can't go back in time.

"Any idea, plan, or purpose may be placed in the mind through repetition of thought."
—Napoleon Hill

"Time" represents progress

Time represents progress; it is nothing but a series of events. We all progress, some slower, some faster, but it's always a forward motion in which we move.

Thought and Its Correct Application

As you move on, drop the baggage you have accumulated during your life on this plane. Lighten your load!

Old hurts are another sore subject. Don't give hurts life by recreating the past, and stop torturing yourself for your past mistakes or dwelling on the idea that others have hurt you. Don't visualize the wrongs; visualize only the beauty and goodness you desire. Look forward, not backward, in all aspects of your life.

Sadness and pain have no place in your experience. Think better thoughts about the situation and see everything as perfect. It will take some practice, but you can only experience what you believe to be true or possible. We are always testing; yes, every experience is just a test.

When you realize who you actually are, your true nature kicks in. You are speaking the truth, so your inert desire starts wanting what's right and good for you. When it feels right, you will want more of it; you want to be right in the mental sense.

"Life will give you whatever experience is most helpful for the evolution of your consciousness. How do you know this is the experience you need? Because this is the experience you are having at the moment."
—Eckhart Tolle

"...because you can!"

How does mentality, mind, and thought work?

Your mind works in a triune fashion: Mind/Cause—Thought/Activity—Effect/Manifestation. Your mind always works from within out.

By this I mean your desire and imagination comes first. The reasoning about your desire, the activity of your thinking, is second. Third, it is reflecting this thinking process into the visible, which occurs after you have made a choice and arrived at a conclusion.

Universal consciousness is at all times in a state of activity or animation. You are part of this Universal consciousness, and your thought or specific mental activity sparks a desire and immediately forms a mental picture. This urge for self-expression naturally starts your desire; this desire, in turn, urges your thought activity to act on it and to express itself into the visible.

Different states of mental activity accompany each problem. Your mentality works in an organized way, systematizing itself naturally from its invisible inception to its visible manifestation. It is an unlabored activity that flows naturally.

Now that you can absolutely control your thoughts, it is necessary to think properly from the starting point of your desire in order to have the ideal outcome.

To reiterate, after you have established an idea or picture of your desire in your mind and reasoned about it, it is absolutely necessary to bring the feeling element into the equation. Know that what you think and feel is fact or the truth. It is the sense or meaning that will be projected into your experience for you to enjoy.

The knowing, the male element of mind, and the feeling, or the female element of mind, must work together in order to produce. It is the mother element, or feeling element, that gives birth to the visible child or idea.

The only thing you can experience is your own knowing and feeling about anything. If you understand how your mind works, you will be able to produce.

> **"Everything is perfect in the universe—even your desire to improve it."**
> —Wayne Dyer

States of Mind

In this state of Unfoldment, we do not go from place to place, but from one mental state to another, higher and higher in the scale of being. We share the same basic purpose in life and for the same reasons. The purpose to enjoy all the good and beauty there is, enjoying more and more of this good as we graduate into the higher states of Universal Consciousness.

> **"All the human traditions and their customs must be sacrificed, given up, and the facts about them understood, if we are to comprehend understanding."**
> —William W. Walter

"...because you can!"

In plain words, man-made traditions in your daily lives and customs regarding home, family, business, and so on must be explored, seen for what they are, and replaced by a higher mental sense and a more refined, loving feeling.

Your motives and life purpose must change. Your reasons for doing certain things will also improve and reflect this newly acquired better sense. Your enthusiasm and good feeling will grow daily as you live your newly energized sense of life.

Practice from your heart, and share what you find with the people that are close to you. That way, your loving sense will spread and help the ones in need.

Your ongoing job in this life is to work on rising to a higher sense of your consciousness and to be more aware of who you really are. You can rise to this higher state by continuous thoughts of truths, learning more about understanding the laws, universal love, and your devotion to life itself.

There is only one Mind. Much has been said about consciousness and the subconscious, one being the "awakened state" and one being the "latent state" of mind. Make no mistake; they are one Mind with two functions.

> **"If you desire many things, many things will seem few."**
> *—Benjamin Franklin*

Be a doer, not a talker

I hear people talk all the time about "what could have," "would have," and "should have" happened. They dwell on the things not accomplished instead of doing what they set out to accomplish.

You might not have succeeded the first time, but you are on your way. If you stick to the basic Laws of the Universe—the Law of Cause and Effect, Law of Like attracts Like, Law of Individuality, and so forth—you will not fail. These laws are discussed in detail in a later chapter.

Remember that the thoughts you think are more important than the trivial, daily things you do. However, your good thoughts must be acted upon to bring them into your experience. Merely talking about them does not do the job.

"You cannot do a kindness too soon, for you never know how soon it will be too late."
—Ralph Waldo Emerson

What contribution can you make to the world?

Every good and right thought will send out a higher frequency contributing to Universal wellness. Helping others, being kind, and teaching how to live a better life is everyone's responsibility. You can help at charities, animal shelters, schools, or just walk someone across the street. Do anything that you would love to be part of.

"...because you can!"

Just remember, don't focus on the wrong within the cause, such as a lack of money or materials in our schools or what others have done wrong within the charitable group. Focus instead on how you can make things better within them and on the good that is already present.

"You can search throughout the entire universe for someone who is more deserving of your love and affection than you are yourself, and that person is not to be found anywhere. You yourself, as much as anybody in the entire universe deserve your love and affection."
—Buddha

Take time for yourself

Rejuvenate. Meditation, taking the time daily to spend in quiet contemplation, is not everyone's cup of tea. However, quiet time is essential to a healthy mind and your well-being. Time spent with yourself and your focused thought, instead of being scattered or absentminded, is part of the cure.

Continue to establish a sense of ease and confidence. In order to think and be happy, you have to make choices, so choose wisely and lovingly. Soften your thoughts about the daily grind, your kids, chores, and work; allow your thoughts to be natural, relaxed, and don't force yourself. It already is good.

Love life and face the knowledge that since you are an individual, it is entirely up to you how your life shapes up, or not. Learn something every day to keep yourself stimulated and excited. Find something that fascinates you, something that you've wanted to try forever. Get up and experience something new...because you can!

"Confidence is that feeling by which the mind embarks in great and honorable courses with a sure hope and trust in itself."
—Marcus Tullius Cicero

ANSWER THESE QUESTIONS HONESTLY:

1. Why do you think the thoughts you think? Do you look at your thought habits and your moods?
2. Could you improve your thoughts? How?
3. Explain the difference between consciousness and the subconscious.
4. How can you get in the habit of focusing on the good instead of the bad?
5. Explain your sense of NOW. Why are past and future not important?
6. How can you control your thoughts?
7. What choices will you make today? What role does choice play?
8. Explain your understanding of male and female elements in the mental.
9. What contribution can you make to the world?
10. What does spending time with yourself look like? Make a list.

CHAPTER 7

FEAR AND DOUBT

Fear and doubt are the greatest deterrents in your search for health, wealth, and happiness. They are bullies not to be believed or trusted.

"We gain strength, and courage, and confidence by each experience in which we really stop to look fear in the face... we must do that which we think we cannot."
—*Eleanor Roosevelt*

When I started to write this chapter, I asked myself what people, including myself, need these days. What are we all looking for? What will help us to improve our life quality? What does everyone yearn for in this time of unrest?

What are our fears? And what are our doubts?

What about you? Do you long for peace, calm, and reassurance? What are your worries and concerns? Are you afraid of everything that comes your way? Is fear your constant companion? Do you have doubt in your heart that all is really good?

I knew I wanted to keep all guidance practical and simple. I didn't want to use pretentious language. I wanted to find an uncomplicated way to explain how altering thought patterns can help change your daily experience. I wanted to get down to the nitty-gritty.

I reasoned that maybe I could give you a different viewpoint, a way of looking at things that would soften the pain. Maybe I could help you to take the edge off life or help relieve whatever sorrow you may be experiencing. I wanted to contribute in making this a better place, a kinder world.

"Be kind whenever possible. It is always possible."
—*Dalai Lama*

What's going on with the thing called "Stress"

Stress is at an all-time high for several reasons: We live in a fast-paced world with little time for contemplation and rest. Violence is a daily occurrence, and unemployment is at its highest since the Great Depression.

Jobs that are available are too often part-time or low paying or represent opportunities in high tech, medical, or bio-engineering fields that require advanced degrees and years of experience.

The job market is highly competitive and, what makes matters worse, education is not everyone's priority as it should be. In many areas of the country, dropout rates are staggering. Young people have little academic or disciplinary supervision due to parents who are either irresponsible or busy dealing with their own problems. They are prone to trouble—joining gangs, missing school, and using drugs.

The divorce rate is at over 50 percent, leaving hundreds of thousands of single mothers to raise children while balancing a full-time job. The uncertain economy, unemployment, and foreclosures challenge family unity, even when families stay together.

Distractions like the Internet, video games, and television tear at the fabric of togetherness. On many levels it seems that life, in general, is a struggle.

From an international aspect, there are nations that lack adequate food and water. We see incredible poverty levels everywhere, including in the United States. Areas of diseases reaching mass proportions and wars with no immediate solutions are everywhere it seems. The help that charitable organizations are providing and all the donations that are sent to the needy areas never seem to be enough.

We are under constant pressure to survive, make a living, raise children under strenuous circumstances, and perform miracles. But where is the balance and enjoyment? Something has to be done. Something has to change...

"...because you can!"

"Be miserable. Or motivate yourself. Whatever has to be done, it's always your choice."
—Wayne Dyer

What has to change?

Having studied for a long time, I have been fortunate to reap the rewards of my labor and experience the fruits of right thinking. I hope that I can give back some of the goodness I receive daily.

I am certain that most people are searching for love; companionship; joy; a healthy, youthful life; a feeling of security; appreciation; self-esteem; and creative, meaningful work. Instinctively, we know that the more of those qualities you have, the more you will enjoy your life and the more fulfilled you will be.

The greatest fears are sickness, poverty, loneliness, fear of failure, fear of not being loved, and, most of all, fear of death. However, there are a large number of smaller fears that need to be addressed before peace of mind can be obtained.

Added to this feeling of fear is the habit of doubting our ability to handle our responsibilities. We doubt that life is good and expect evil. We doubt that we have abundance and experience poverty. We doubt that we are loved and feel loneliness.

What has to change is your *expectancy* of the possibility to experience negativity.

Your *expectancy* must change to a sense of having only positive experiences.

Lift your outlook to a more optimistic view. Eliminate the doubt that something will go wrong; anticipate only the good.

"There is nothing more dreadful than the habit of doubt. Doubt separates people. It is a poison that disintegrates friendships and breaks up pleasant relations. It is a thorn that irritates and hurts; it is a sword that kills."
—Buddha

Everything you have learned from the day you were born was a lie

Starting with "your body is solid" and "you are a material being," everything you were taught is pretty much incorrect.

Your belief that you are a material being capable of hurt and disease causes additional stress and fear. It is time for you to forget yourself as a person. Take the standpoint that all of life is mental, and that you are a mental being.

Yes, you are a mental being. You are a Soul. You are Spirit.

Your fears were instilled in you by your parents, teachers, guides, doctors, and peers, starting from the day you were born. Those fears continue to be reinforced by a 24/7 news cycle that preaches impending disaster, illness, violence, and economic collapse. Fear sells!

As a baby, you were afraid of being abandoned by your parents. You cried when your mother left you in the crib and walked away. As a child, you were afraid of imaginary monsters and scary, bigger things because you were little. As a teenager, you were afraid of not fitting in or being too ugly for the boy/girl next door. You also feared not fitting in socially at school, or not being popular, or not having the right wardrobe or body type.

The countless fears of loneliness, of being hurt or getting injured, and most of all the I fear of the *possibility* of having bad things happen to you, is endless.

A helpful exercise is to make a list of all of the fears you have ever experienced at different stages of life, fears you had just last year, last month, and last week. Write down fears about work, bills, health, family, housing, or anything else that burdens you now.

**"Worry never robs tomorrow of its sorrow,
it only saps today of its joy."
—Leo Buscaglia**

All fears are man-made; that is, they're imagined by us. They are unreal, self-induced, and the opposite of good. Fear is just waiting to creep up on you when you least expect it.

Fear and Doubt

There is no running away from fear. There is only one solution. We have to face our fears; we cannot sweep them under the rug. We cannot escape them without addressing the issues. We have to deal with them and dissolve the terrifying feeling of fear and anxiety through reason and understanding.

Think of fear as "sin." The word "sin" means to "miss the mark." So when we sin, we only miss the mark; we make a mistake. This just means we did not act as appropriately as we should have.

So when we are afraid of something, we are sinning, or missing the mark, because we believe that there is something out there other than good. We believe that something can hurt us. By accepting the lies—that we are mere, material humans—we become vulnerable to those imaginary fears.

We can correct our wrong thoughts immediately, and we must. We must think fearless, positive, and good thoughts, and we must act good no matter what the situation or fear.

If good is all there is, and the Universe is composed of perfect Intelligence, then evil, or anything lesser than good, cannot be real. It is the opposite and can only be a lack of good or a wrong sense that needs correction.

> **"Fear defeats more people than any other one thing in the world."**
> —*Ralph Waldo Emerson*

The fear of losing your job

Any time, but especially in this economy, the fear of losing your job is tremendous. It is chilling. People consider jobs to be essential to their lifestyle and the sole source of income. People, then, will act according to their beliefs, thinking it *is* the only source of income. This, in turn, will cause it to be this way.

Because they believe they are dependent on the job, they become extremely anxious. They mistakenly think the job is necessary for survival, and it appears exactly as expected, as people are the cause of all that they experience.

In addition to this stressful thinking, people are convinced they cannot survive without a job or monetary income.

Remember the Law of Cause and Effect. Whatever you believe in your heart to be true will be true in *your* reality, but this does not mean it is true in actuality.

Now, because of the belief that this job is the sole source of income, the termination or loss of this job seems devastating and seems like a "separation" from familiar things. The ability to provide for themselves and their loved ones has been taken away, or so it seems.

It's the same with anything, whether it's a loss of a certain possession, a loss of a relationship, and so forth. It seems people have no control over their destiny. No wonder the anxiety level of many people is so high.

"Some changes look negative on the surface but you will soon realize that space is being created in your life for something new to emerge."
—Eckhart Tolle

To improve this terrifying sense of fear, you have to change your perception about the situation.

Start seeing the loss of job, loss of relationships, or any other loss as a necessary change or push in the right direction. It is provided to you by Universal Intelligence. It is necessary for your progress, even though you see it as disastrous, completely calamitous, and think it is the end of all.

Most people can tell you, myself included, that after the first shock of losing your job, other doors will open. Looking back, it will prove to you that it was a necessary push to get you to move on to a new venture. If you allow it, it will certainly help your progress.

From a perceptive viewpoint, it looks like a "loss of," but from a mental viewpoint, it was a step to greater understanding, testing, learning, and growth.

Ultimately, it is a journey of the Soul. You will learn to have courage, patience, persistence, endurance, strength—all wonderful qualities of the mind.

"Inaction breeds doubt and fear. Action breeds confidence and courage. If you want to conquer fear, do not sit home and think about it. Go out and get busy."
—Dale Carnegie

"...because you can!"

The "hurry, worry disease"

Fear is a liar. It terrifies and distorts. Fear is an intense, wrong feeling.

A lesser sense of fear would be hurry and worry. The following: "Hurry!", "Rush!", or "Don't wait—act now!" Advertising campaigns send these messages to us every day. "C'mon, let's go!" is what we've been programmed to say the minute the light turns green and the car ahead of us hasn't moved. We feel the same way when we have to sit for an extra second or two as our computer downloads information we believe we need...immediately!

We think we constantly have to be on the run because we fear being late. Notice how we always have to run to some place; we are always on the go.

This running around is a wrong sense, thinking that you are not getting things done in time. You are constantly thinking that you are missing something somewhere.

What are you missing? What will happen if you stop and smell the roses?

We need to ask ourselves these questions: What is the rush? When do we take a moment, even a quick one, to understand there is time for everything worthwhile if we allow ourselves to take that time for ourselves and our spirit?

Fear and Doubt

Certainly, some deadlines cannot be avoided, or emergencies arise and time matters more than anything. Yet, such occasions are not day to day.

The truth is, we have all the time in the world. Just do one thing at a time, and go on calmly with your daily business. This relaxed state of mind will save you the time you think you don't have.

Worry is also a fear about all the smaller things in life. The kids are not home from school yet, and you worry about their safety. The bills haven't been paid, and you worry if there are enough funds in the bank. A relative isn't doing too well, and you worry if she will be cured anytime soon. Any kind of uneasiness that creeps up in your consciousness steadily is an unnecessary worry. Many people worry about everything.

Basically, all discomfort and bad experiences in life, when truly analyzed, stem from fear. The feeling element within you is the mother element and a magnifier, multiplying the fears. The more wrong feeling, the more fear.

To worry about something is useless. It doesn't solve the problem; it only magnifies it and makes you uneasy, tense, and sick. You can't sleep and are in constant strain. Your anxiety levels are extremely high. What an unhealthy way to live!

Heal yourself of unnecessary mental pain, worry, doubt, and fear by reasoning about the truth and by diligent, right thinking. This right thinking includes calm

"...because you can!"

and comforting thoughts and reassuring yourself that all is good and will work out alright in accordance to the Law. Trust in the Allness of Good. Know that Life is Love. Love is the opposite of Fear.

All obstacles are only opportunities to learn and test yourself and your Understanding of the Allness of Good. The healing occurs when you let go of the unreasonable worries and see more good in your life instead of hurdles.

You are a creator, you are powerful, and you are in charge of your life. You are Love, Strength, Courage, and Life, and don't let anyone or anything tell you differently!

"Fear doesn't exist anywhere except in the mind."
—Dale Carnegie

Fear of aging

The beauty industry is thriving. Cosmetics have become all too common in our society. And instead of creating it ourselves, we allowed the beauty industry to define for us physical perfection. We allowed someone else to dictate what is appealing and acceptable.

I live fifteen minutes from Beverly Hills, California, where there are thousands of plastic surgeons. A study commissioned by the American Society for Aesthetic Plastic Surgery shows that in 2010, 53 percent of women and 49 percent of men said they approve of cosmetic surgery. Women had nearly 8.6 million cosmetic procedures (92 percent of the total), and men had more than 750,000 procedures (8 percent of the total).

Having plastic surgery in itself is not wrong; it's similar to maintaining your car. You get yourself tuned up every so often, which is a blessing for victims of accidents or violent crimes; it's a lifesaver for children born with birth defects and disfigurations.

However, having a procedure because you are insecure and don't like yourself or the way you look is a wrong reason for this course of action. Wanting to look like someone else is detrimental. You are an individual, and your appearance only reflects your character and what you think of yourself.

Wanting to look younger, more youthful, can be accomplished by having a more youthful attitude and better outlook in life.

Aging is not "getting older"; it is maturing and should be enjoyed to the fullest. You have acquired wisdom; you have experience, and you know what you want. So make the most out of it and enjoy it.

Enjoy everything you know; you've earned it!

Keep yourself active. It is never too late to start anew: a new career, a new relationship, a new hobby. Now is the time to do what you've always wanted to do. And most of all, a new, young, vibrant attitude will certainly reflect on the body.

> **"Old age, believe me, is a good and pleasant thing. It is true you are gently shouldered off the stage, but then you are given such a comfortable front stall as spectator."**
> **—Confucius**

Fear of sickness

Fear is also a big part of all human ailments and sickness—a huge contributor to diseases.

Erring belief in sickness, or plain ignorance coupled with the supposition that you have no power over sickness, is a false belief. It is a mental conviction in the reality of anything lesser than good.

I am pointing out again that the male and the female (knowing and feeling) elements must both be present in the mentality before expression to any condition is given. So think and feel healthy and well at all times, no matter what the appearance.

To have absolutely no fear of the disease is to be utterly immune to it. Just think of all the doctors and nurses working in hospitals, for example, or caretakers of the elderly. Being afraid of any kind of disease makes us subject to it.

There are countless fears in everyone when it comes to sickness, from the fear of cold weather giving you a cold to the tremendous and, of course, understandable fear of dying from cancer.

Fear and Doubt

The healing of any kind of disease (or uneasiness) is natural and will follow when right thinking is applied. This right thinking should, of course, be accompanied by a responsible way of living. It should include a well-balanced diet, exercise or yoga and meditation, medical checkups, and refraining from smoking, excessive alcohol use, and drugs.

In reality, sickness is the effect of wrong or sick thought and can also be healed by thought correction. The world at large is still ignorant to the fact that sickness is caused by sick or wrong, unhealthy thoughts that persist over time. I have included some examples in the Well-being chapter.

True healing is mental in nature and must be accomplished by changing your mental attitude to include health consciousness. Healing will be achieved when you can see your true nature as being spirit, mental. See yourself as the SOUL you are—not a physical, material being.

Thinking wholesome, good thoughts will make you healthy and good. We must think in conformity with Universal Truth. The truth is that everything already is perfect and well, and you are part of this Universal Perfection. Sickness is not part of this Universal Perfection nor is it part of the natural state of being.

Wellness and Health are your natural state.

"...because you can!"

> "The whole secret of existence is to have no fear. Never fear what will become of you, depend on no one. Only the moment you reject all help are you freed."
> —**Buddha**

The real cause of fear

The real cause of all fear is ignorance, or not knowing the facts of life. It is being unaware of the Truth that life is eternal. It is pure mental darkness. Fear comes from the belief that you are a victim—not a victor—and that you have no power over your state of health, wealth, and happiness.

It takes Intelligence to destroy this ignorance; it takes learning to gain knowledge; it takes reason to come to a sound conclusion; it takes patience; and, most of all, it takes courage.

> "There is nothing that wastes the body like worry, and one who has any faith in God should be ashamed to worry about anything whatsoever."
> —**Mohandas Gandhi**

Conclusion

To sum it up, fear the greatest of all sins; it is the expectancy of evil, destruction, and death. It is your expectancy that something will go wrong or something will hurt you and your loved ones. It is your ex-

Fear and Doubt

pectancy of misfortunes and that death will end all. These assumptions are self-destructive.

After getting involved in the study of life, many people have great success in their newfound power of thought. They acquire things they desire, and their lives become more relaxed and enjoyable. However, the slightest mishaps spiral them right back to doubt, which, in turn, causes fear. You will alleviate fear only by sincerely dealing with all areas and casting out doubt of possible failures and disappointments. You have to start somewhere.

Remember that you are not alone and out to fend for yourself. You are a particle of Universal Intelligence and Power. Always think of yourself as fearless and powerful. Have courage because you are a creator. Life is not meant to be dreadful and hard; it is meant to be enjoyed. Do not judge according to appearances; they are false, phenomena only, and don't jump to conclusions without proper reasoning.

Understanding is the true fear remover and destroyer.

"We are not victims of aging, sickness and death. These are part of scenery, not the seer, who is immune to any form of change. This seer is the spirit, the expression of eternal being."
—Deepak Chopra

Muster up all your courage and fight this bully of fear...because you can!

ANSWER THESE QUESTIONS HONESTLY:

1. Is fear your constant companion?
2. What are your major fears?
3. What are you looking for in this time of unrest?
4. Do you doubt your abilities and talents? Why?
5. Do you doubt that ALL is really good? Why?
6. Make a list of fears that burden you now.
7. Why do you hurry and worry? Make a list.
8. Can you see that sickness is caused by sick thinking?
9. What's the healer?
10. What will remove fear and doubt? Why?

CHAPTER 8

APPRECIATION AND GRATITUDE

"Appreciation is the highest form of prayer, for it acknowledges the presence of good wherever you shine the light of your thankful thoughts."
—Alan Cohen

Wake up every morning "giving thanks"

Give thanks for the blessings you have received and for the blessings that are coming your way today and every day. Saying "thank you" to the Universe with sincere appreciation puts you instantly into a positive frame of mind. Gratefulness will catapult you to a higher frequency and will trigger loving thoughts naturally.

"...because you can!"

Pay attention to your thoughts first thing in the morning

Are you waking up smiling, ready to enjoy a day at work, ready to stroll through a park, jog at the beach, or meet a friend for lunch? Are you ready to embrace your children and your spouse or significant other? Are you prepared to love and act kindly? Are you excited to see a new day and look forward to new adventures? Are you ready to learn?

Or, are you unhappy and resentful the minute you open your eyes? Are you miserable already, even though you haven't put on your clothes yet? Do you dread going to work or resent not having work to go to, spending the day with an elderly family member? Are you still upset over a meaningless argument from the night before? Are you bored and don't know what to do with yourself today or any day?

How does your day shape up? Is it all that you want it to be? Does it come close to your ideal?

Here is a lovely "thanksgiving" prayer:

"Now we turn our thoughts to the Creator, or Great Spirit, and send greetings and thanks for the gifts of Creation. Everything we need to live a good life is here on this Mother Earth. For all the love that is still around us, we gather our minds together as one and send our choicest words of greetings and thanks to the Creator."
—*Haudenosaunee*

Appreciation and Gratitude

Now that you've discovered that you are the cause of your daily experiences, you can be grateful that you are in charge of your life. You can be exuberant not having to depend on anyone or anything outside of yourself.

Keep in mind that everything is mental and everything is good. You are the arbiter of your own fate. Your thought counts from the first awakening, starting in the morning, to your last thought before you fall asleep.

Even while sleeping, your subconscious is working, digesting and systematizing your day's experiences and impressions. It will register the mood encountered while dozing off. Going to sleep with a grateful heart will let you rest a lot better than a worried and disturbed mind.

Say "thank you" to the Universe or source of all being before you drift away. Know the next day will be even better and greater, and you will be closer to your goal of happiness.

I would suggest a daily, short "ritual" of saying thank you. Maybe you want to do this with soft, soothing music, flickering candles, or incense in the evenings to relax after a busy day. During the warm days of summer, an open window releasing a gentle breeze might be a good way to show your appreciation. You can give thanks in a secluded place in stillness, or you can shout it out loud. Let your heart speak.

You might just look in the mirror in the morning and say thank you to yourself for your diligent study, your kindness, your good intentions, and your love for being alive.

> **"Something opens our wings. Something makes boredom and hurt disappear. Someone fills the cup in front of us: We taste only sacredness."**
> —*Rumi*

What to watch for

Watch yourself during the day and listen to your inner dialogue. Do you easily get discouraged or angry? Does your temper rise quickly? What triggers your mood to change?

Are you grateful for the meal you ate and the hot shower this morning? Do you appreciate the warm bed and the roof over your head, or do you take all of this for granted? Do you feel it's a struggle, that you're just getting by and it's not enough?

The surest way to a better life is through gratitude and an appreciation of even the smallest things.

Thank the Universe for its generosity, and look at Nature and its bounty with a sense of awe. See the flowers and the creatures, the sunshine and the raindrops in their glory. Try it now. Do you feel the love pouring down from the heavens and embracing you with its song?

On a mental level, give thanks to the fact that in reality your consciousness knows all there is to know. You have only forgotten who you really are and are in the process of remembering your true nature. You, not being fully aware of this fact, are on your way to unfold this knowledge from within.

No matter your present circumstances, acknowledge and be grateful that you are not a helpless human being, struggling to survive. You, at this point of your unfoldment, know that you can change your situation according to your sense about the situation.

You are made of Universal substance: Wisdom, Goodness, and Intelligence. Your true nature is mental in origin.

It is your Soul that does the living, not your body. Your body is the visible expression of your Soul. So be grateful for the body you have, and treat it with respect and kindness. It is the only body you have here on this plane, and it should be treasured.

> **"Choosing to be positive and having a grateful attitude is going to determine how you're going to live your life."**
> **—Joel Osteen**

What about the unpleasant experiences? Should you be grateful for those?

It's easy to be thankful for good things, but what about things and situations that "look" bad?

"...because you can!"

Here is a story of a lady that surely thought she had reason to be angry and hurt.

But did she?

Aileen's Story

"I worked for a mid-sized company as an executive assistant to the president for fourteen years. I started out as a receptionist and, as my job responsibilities and title changed, I was always told by the president that he would basically have my back and 'look out for me' forever.

"I rented my duplex from the company and lived there for sixteen years. I was told, after the first ten years or so, not to worry about it being sold or having to relocate as I would always have first option to buy the place and I would be given a very good price. Even after I quit working for the company, given my close professional relationship over the years with my ex-boss and president, he assured me, time and time again, that I would never have to worry about moving, that I would be 'taken care of.'

"One Friday I received a phone call from my former employer and he told me that the duplex was going on the market. I asked when and he told me it was going on the market that very same afternoon. No warning. No prior notice. It was simply a nonchalant phone call asking me to allow the realtors to show my place. There was never any mention

Appreciation and Gratitude

of any 'gentlemen's agreement' or any tip of the hand that the monies I had paid for sixteen years of renting would count for anything towards purchasing the house.

"I was stunned, hurt, and angry and grew increasingly bitter once I realized I had been lied to. It was an awful time for me—very emotional and hurtful—and the anger I had was intense and ugly. I ended up making an offer on the house, only to have my former boss continue to undermine my attempts to buy it and bolster up the price to create a bidding war with other potential buyers. I hired a lawyer and was told by my former boss that he would drag the proceedings out till I had exhausted all my monies on attorney fees.

"Bitter and defeated, I bought a condo and moved to the valley. In retrospect, of course, it was the best thing that happened to me. I proved I could buy a house on my own, dependent on no one but myself and my own resourcefulness. I 'blamed' my former boss for all my woes and troubles, but, in truth, I was responsible for all my decisions and needed to step up to the plate and own them.

"I know that now, and that is when the waves of appreciation washed over me. Grateful to let all that negativity leave. Grateful to be self-sufficient. Appreciative for all that I had learned in the process. Truly, it opened my eyes and led the way for me to trek down a much more positive path than the one I had been wandering."

"And isn't discontent the lever of change?"
—*John Steinbeck*

Here is another very common example:

Let's say you've just lost your job. You are shocked and confused, and you don't know what to do right now. Can you appreciate that losing your job will open new doors and bring you new opportunities?

Maybe you are sick and have been ailing for some time. Can you appreciate that it is nature's way of showing you that you need to make a change in your lifestyle, thinking, or character? Can you be grateful for that?

A friend of mine was laid off in her midforties and was devastated at the unexpected life change. She worked for a licensing group and dealt with product placement. For several years before this lay off she had helped out in my special events department at a Hollywood movie studio as a part-time designer and decorator.

She was very talented, and I could see how much she enjoyed doing this kind of work. Her husband and I asked her one day what she would really like to do if she could, and she said that she would love to go back to school and become a "real" designer. We had this conversation almost a year before she was laid off.

Here was her opportunity. Jobless and ready to move on with her life, she enrolled in design school at the age of forty-five. Being without that steady paycheck and the security of full-time employment was unsettling to her. However, she worked relentlessly on the fulfillment of her dream, and she graduated with a bachelor's degree in interior design from Interior Designer's Institute in Newport Beach, at the top of her class!

Today she has a design firm, and she is happier than ever, all because she was laid off and was pushed to make a change. She would never have made this transition and decision on her own. Talk about being grateful for having turned around a seemingly devastating situation!

"Everyone has been made for some particular work, and the desire for that work has been put in every heart."
—*Rumi*

When you feel down and discouraged

Find things that you can be grateful for, no matter how small. I know it's not always easy, especially on days of despair.

Like anything else, it gets easier with practice, and it will keep your focus on what's right rather than on what's wrong. Here is another opportunity for you to make a list of big and little things in life that warrant appreciation every day. Putting it on paper will put it in perspective, and you will see the importance of appreciation.

"...because you can!"

"What is going on inside me?" is a good question to ask yourself when you feel angry or lonely or just plain miserable. Do you wonder why you feel the way you feel? Is it a habit? Plain carelessness? What triggers it, and what makes you tick?

> **"Happiness is not something ready made.
> It comes from your own actions."**
> —*Dalai Lama*

The "black hole"

At one time or another, we have all experienced that vicious cycle between habitual wrong thoughts and raw emotions. They feed each other, and the downward spiral begins. I call it the "black hole."

You can feel the "black hole" coming on when all of a sudden your mood changes. Something triggers you to jump back to an old hurt or disappointment, jealousy, or resentment. You're not quite sure what made you think of this occurrence, but suddenly and unwittingly you experience this knot in your stomach, and you mire in negative emotions. You recall instantaneously the negative emotions this incident had at the time.

When I feel myself getting close to the "black hole," I stop and consciously find something I love, which could be just talking to my animals, looking at the flowers in my garden, or calling my husband or a friend to hear a familiar voice.

When I do call someone to vent, I do not call to complain about my woes, thereby making things more real and giving them more power. I call to change the subject within my "not so good" and disturbed thoughts. I only look for positive support and reinforcement.

It might be good for you to go out for a walk and observe nature. Check out a book at the library, and be grateful for the librarian who helped you find the novel on the shelves. Sing a favorite song. Write a letter, not an e-mail, to a special someone. Anything that turns your attention from negative thoughts.

Continuously dwelling on the wrong situation or person feeds energy into the emotion, which in turn energizes the wrong thought pattern. As I said, it's a vicious cycle. Stop these feelings when you feel them coming on.

"Knowing your own darkness is the best method for dealing with the darkness of other people."
—Carl Jung

Believe it or not, bad experiences are really good. They are a lesson; they are what you need to progress at the time. They are blessings.

How do you turn the black hole into a radiant circle of light?

We turn the black hole upside down by refusing to fall into it. You have a choice: you can either continue

"...because you can!"

to dwell on the past and the thoughts that led up to your mood, or you can say "No, I will not think such wrong thoughts again." You can acknowledge the situation, feelings, and emotions for what they are, or you can continue to suffer. It is up to you.

How grateful we should be to be able to switch unpleasant things around. We only have to change our view the situation.

Each experience helps to complete the puzzle if Life is to be complete.

Each challenge that is solved by you is necessary to make you whole. So the black hole exists to point out areas in your thinking that are still dark and unresolved.

In this process of unfoldment, we have found that Synchronicity plays a big part in our daily lives. It is this Universal synchronic plan that helps you solve the puzzle. You have to listen and look around you and act on the clues.

"What the caterpillar calls the end of the world the master calls a butterfly."
—*Richard Bach*

Synchronicity

I know it's hard to believe, but there are no coincidences or accidents.

Appreciation and Gratitude

Everything in the Universe is perfectly orchestrated. Synchronicity is the seeming coincidence of events that appear to be related, even though they are not caused by one or the other. It is a situation in which two or more things happen at the same time and seem to be connected, even if they are not. The term was first used in this sense in the world of the psychologist Carl Jung.

Let me tell you a little story on how life works and synchronicity at its best.

When I was in my twenties, working for a record company in Germany, I never imagined that one day I would live in America. I had never even thought about it. A musician myself, I toured with bands and traveled all over Europe. I loved my life as it was exciting and ever changing.

In the winter of 1981, I saw Al Jarreau in London with friends who represented his German record label at the time.

One evening our group met in the lobby of the hotel. Al waved me over to his table and, out of the blue, said, "You should go to Hollywood. You really would fit in." I told him that I never thought about it and had no desire, but he insisted and said again, "You really should go to Hollywood."

Something stuck and, a couple of weeks later on an icy cold Hamburg day, I booked a ten-day trip, arriving at LAX in eighty-degree weather, where the palm trees were swaying, and I jumped on a bus and made my way to Hollywood. The rest is history. After thirty years, I am still in this great city. Everything fell into place naturally thereafter.

I never saw Al Jarreau again and, after all this time, I can truly say that I am the most thankful person for his insight.

Without his comment, my own instinctive reaction, and my acting upon it, I would not be here in this country that I love so much. Providing you with opportunities and possibilities, synchronicity is life's organized map. You just have to listen and act.

"A man sooner or later discovers that he is the master-gardener of his soul, the director of his life."
—James Allen

Ask yourself, "What does my world look like right now?"

The next question should be this: "How do I want my life to look?"

You now know that your thought governs your reality. We, being part of this Universal source, are showing ourselves the pictures from which we have to learn. We are causing events that are guiding us in a new direction, whenever necessary.

Watch the little things, like a message on the TV that catches your eye, a book that opens at a certain

Appreciation and Gratitude

page, a letter in the junk mail that you would normally throw in the trash. These are clues.

You might run into a person you haven't seen in a long time, remembering that he or she practiced law. All of a sudden, a relative dies and you need an estate attorney. Thankful to have reconnected, you call this friend, and it turns out to be a perfect match.

"Life is what happens to you while you're busy making other plans."
—John Lennon

Not too long ago, I received a phone call from a lady I knew from my previous job. We had done business together for many years, but personally I didn't know her very well. She worked for a publishing company and I was her client, having contact with her maybe twice a year.

After the layoff from my company, I had the urge to talk to her, which was unusual as I didn't have a personal connection to her; and so I invited her to have coffee. Mind you, I had never asked her out before. We chatted casually, exchanged numbers, and on we went.

Several weeks later, she called and asked me to join her in a meeting. The owner of the company needed an experienced person that would develop their events department. I wasn't looking for a job, nor did I want to go back into this type of work. I resisted and told them no, not once but three times.

"...because you can!"

At one point, I realized that the Universe was trying to tell me something. I wasn't listening, but I needed to start paying attention. I finally went to check it out and, to my surprise, it was the perfect opportunity.

Several months previously, I had outlined my desire for the perfect job. I had in detail described all that needed to be present in order for me to go back to work. And here it was. Again, I only had to listen and act. It led to the perfect business opportunity. It was a chance of a lifetime, and we sealed the deal.

Repeat after me: there are no coincidences and accidents. A great synchronized plan is in store for each of us, shapeable by our desires and its fulfillment through right thought, supported by the Universe's perfect plan.

> **"Doing what you love is the cornerstone of having abundance in your life."**
> —Wayne Dyer

Life is good

Life is good—that's the bottom line! If you experience anything less than good, take responsibility. Get started and change what needs to be corrected. And yes, you start with appreciating that which you already have. I am sure when you really think about it, you can find many, many things.

In your search for the perfect life, don't blame yourself for your past mistakes. You did the best you could

Appreciation and Gratitude

with the tools given, relative to your understanding. Now you know better, and you appreciate this knowledge. This, in turn, will bring you more Understanding, a better existence.

With this grateful heart, go out into the world and spread the good word. Don't preach or impose yourself on others. Rather, share your knowledge and good fortune. Don't force your beliefs on others, but walk the talk. Demonstrate positive change by example.

Be helpful and kind. Practice small kindnesses like writing a "thank you" note. Tell someone else other than your family and friends that you love them, and offer a small gift of appreciation. The gift of your time speaks volumes as well. Do a favor by offering a helping hand.

We have to become a less self-absorbed, more kinder nation by appreciating the good we are blessed with and sharing more good with all living beings.

"I dreamed I was a butterfly, flitting around in the sky; then I awoke. Now I wonder: Am I a man who dreamt of being a butterfly, or am I a butterfly dreaming that I am a man?"
—*Zhuangzi*

Now, it's time to move forward and soar. Be that beautiful butterfly and appreciate thyself, thy neighbors, and thy Universe...because you can!

Thank you!

ANSWER THESE QUESTIONS HONESTLY:

1. Do you appreciate the life you have?
2. Do you give thanks every day?
3. Do you wake up happy in the morning? What causes your mood to change?
4. What is going on inside of you?
5. What makes you happy or sad, and what triggers certain reactions?
6. How do you turn the "black hole" into a radiant circle of light?
7. How do you want your life to look?
8. What nice gesture of appreciation can you show someone today?
9. What do you appreciate the most?
10. Do you appreciate yourself?

CHAPTER 9

MENTAL WORK

What does mental work mean?

"Work" does not only imply employment, going to work, cleaning the house, or doing other chores. It is your daily *mental* work that should be every bit as important, or even more important, than your daily physical work.

"The main purpose of life is to live rightly, think rightly, act rightly. The soul must languish when we give all our thought to the body."
—*Mohandas Gandhi*

We all agree that practice makes perfect, so work on making right thinking, which is right mental work, a habit. By continuous practice, your subconscious will absorb your affirmations and act accordingly. It will take some diligent effort and plenty of repetition to establish the new thought concepts. However, you will reap the positive rewards of its effects, results that will reaffirm the correctness of your exercises. Any time invested will be well worth it.

With a satisfied mind comes rest and joy. When your mind is operating with calm confidence, knowing that what you've accomplished is for your good and the good of all, the fruits of your labor will manifest in your daily experiences. Your sense of calm and joy is your reward for diligent, correct mental work.

As each problem is solved, your mentality rests. Forgotten are the struggles and obstacles, and peace is yours.

> **"One does not need buildings, money, power, or status to practice the Art of Peace. Heaven is right where you are standing, and that is the place to train."**
> **—Morihei Ueshiba**

What is rest?

Most everyone thinks that rest is a physical action. This is not so. To think that physical action can make you tired is wrong. Yes, you will feel tired after a long workout or rigorous work schedule, but this fatigue is a mental sense. This mental association of doing work is what made you tired.

The body itself never knew the difference to begin with. Only your mind knew what you where doing. Your mind processed that you were performing so-called work, and it was you, your mind that associated a certain kind of work with getting tired or needing rest.

The body is not conscious and, therefore, cannot sense being tired. Only your mentality can do so. Your belief of work making you tired creates this sensation.

Think about a sleepless night that you've experienced in the past. Your body might have been lying down, but your mind was active and restless. You felt tired in the morning. Shouldn't your body have been rested since it was lying down?

No, it felt tired because only your mind is conscious; therefore, only your mind can feel the restlessness you experienced. The battleground is always your consciousness. All work is mental.

"Learn from yesterday, live for today, hope for tomorrow. The important thing is not to stop questioning."
—*Albert Einstein*

There will always be "something" you need to work on

Never stop questioning. Question all your actions and your thoughts. Your own intelligence, which will not let you get away with anything, will always present you with the challenges you need to improve yourself.

Any obstacles, sufferings, or unpleasant experiences of any kind are usually nothing more than a test of your understanding. They are a kick in the butt to get you up and going, telling you to go on with your unfoldment.

Don't coast, and don't be lazy or shiftless. Your progress is the most important thing in your life.

A new challenge, a new venture, or a new test will always present itself. But life moves forward, and since you are part of this life, you will never be stagnant. Just make sure you are moving in the right direction—always upward.

"Why should I ask the wise men: Whence is my beginning? I am busy with the thought: Where will be my end?"
—Muhammad Iqbal

Work on yourself

When you look in the mirror, you see what you have temporarily concluded of yourself. Like it or not, this is what you think of yourself. If you don't like the reflection, both physically and mentally, your work is to change and improve it and better yourself.

If you like what you see, good job, but there is always room for improvement.

It is helpful to write down your daily thoughts in a journal. It will show you a pattern of behavior and emotions. I find that when I jot down quick thoughts in times of distress and doubt, by the end of the day,

Mental Work

most of those concerns have vanished. When you see your woes on paper, they are more tangible, more manageable, and less scary.

Your mind and your imagination have a tendency to run wild if not controlled by reason. Making the effort to focus on those thoughts by writing them down will release some of the anxiety; it will seem that you are getting a "hold on" yourself.

> **"Writing, to me, is simply thinking through my fingers."**
> *—Isaac Asimov*

It has been long established that walking and exercise are great tools to relieve your pent up steam. It clears your mind.

I have never been one to enjoy a rigorous workout but have found that a brisk, early morning walk around my neighborhood does wonders to start the day fresh. It helps me focus before starting a day of work. Find something that works and benefits you, something that is refreshing and helps you to cope with your daily responsibilities.

It is very important that you work on yourself and get your life in order, because if you are not happy or healthy, how could you help someone else to be happy or healthy?

> **"Behavior is what a man does, not what he thinks, feels, or believes."**
> *—Emily Dickinson*

Our work with others

Besides the mental work we do within ourselves, we are also working with others, especially in the physical work environment. We always come into contact with others. We mentally think of them, imagine them, and sense them, but we also have bodily and verbal contact as we work with them.

In our relationship with others, we are involved with their day-to-day experiences. However, we are usually so self-absorbed that we mostly function and provide for ourselves and the closest of family and friends.

It is wonderful to talk to and encourage your friends and family and rewarding to be a good companion and parent. It is imperative to spend time with your children and be interested in their lives as it is our work to raise and prepare them for life. (Don't dictate. Just observe and, with your good thoughts and support, they will blossom like the Universe intended them to.)

But you would also contribute to the Universal good by endeavoring to help someone less fortunate. Spend time, for example, with people that are lonely, or volunteer at a hospital or charity. Get involved in something that helps others to live a better life.

"Love begins at home, and it is not how much we do... but how much love we put in that action."
—Mother Teresa

How to cope with a hectic schedule in the physical work place?

What I call "the hamster" is in all of our minds. The wheel is constantly spinning, and it seems that you are running forever in the same place.

Do you feel you never have time for everything you want to do? Are you overloading yourself with all kinds of errands and responsibilities that might not be necessary?

Is your job fulfilling? Is it challenging? Do you feel happy or stressed on a daily basis? Are you over doing it? Or on the opposite side of the spectrum, are you a shiftless procrastinator?

In a perfect world, everyone has the perfect job, job they love and happily go to every morning. In this desirable world, one wouldn't have a profession or career that's boring or unappealing.

If your occupation is work that you love, the QUALITY of the work naturally will improve because it is done by you with interest and care. When you come home to your loved ones after a day's work, you'd be happy to see them. You'd be satisfied with your accomplishments at work and have a smile on your face. Your family would be grateful for your pleasant attitude and the quality of your family life would improve also.

Life is a circle, and everything is interlocked and works naturally.

"...because you can!"

> **"Peace comes from within. Do not seek it without."**
> *—Buddha*

How is the quality of your work?

Are you satisfied with the work you produce or the service you give to your clients? Think about what the word *quality* means to you. Can you maintain your thoughts of the highest quality you can sense?

High mental qualities like patience, kindness, peace, harmony, honesty, as well as earthly qualities like being on time, a pleasant tone of voice, politeness, cleanliness, being considerate when driving, and so forth are necessary.

Your work is part of your self-expression. Self-expression is mental. You can express yourself in many ways and produce beautiful things. You can communicate through writing, and you can sell enjoyable goods, invent useful items, or define yourself in many other productive and creative ways.

Everything you do in your work is part of that self-expression. Always look and see if you can include being of service to others. How can others benefit from what you are offering? How can they enjoy your work or product?

> **"Quality is not an act, it is a habit."**
> *—Aristotle*

Connect with your co-workers in a positive way

In your workplace, it is best to not react to co-workers or take things personally, including the attitudes and criticisms of superiors. It is much better to stay positive and be a good sport and promote camaraderie. Be respectful and helpful, but stay away from gossip and personal drama.

Keep in mind that people around you are just as perfect as you are, no matter what the appearance. They are mental beings coming from the same source, possessing the same inherent qualities. Again, it's their actions or character that can be faulty—not their soul.

Enjoy the people around you; they are a reflection of you, your qualities, and your faults.

> **"How people treat you is their karma;
> how you react is yours."
> —Wayne Dyer**

Compensation

Regarding your income, or what looks to be your paycheck, keep your sense right about your worth. Know in your heart that you will be compensated plentifully and generously because you are giving good service or are promoting excellent products. Give 110 percent while at work and enjoy what you do while doing it.

"...because you can!"

Even if the appearance is the opposite, you have to keep a sense of abundance. Your paycheck might still reflect a shortage of funds, but you have to imagine having plenty and keep your faith strong. (More on this in the Abundance chapter.)

Know that you are valuable, and keep a high sense of yourself.

"If you are not being treated with respect, check your price tag. Perhaps you have marked yourself down. It's you who tells people what you are worth by what you accept. Get off the clearance rack and get behind the glass where the valuables are kept! Learn to value yourself more, because if you don't no one else will!"
—Mary Johnson

Supply comes from within you, not from an outside source. It looks like the paycheck comes from your employer, but you are your supply, your resource. You are providing for yourself through your abundant thinking. Your sense of wealth and your excellent mental qualities are the providers.

You can make plenty of money because income is really "outgo." It is your creative contribution "going out" from your mentality's activity to the visible world.

If you are in the process of looking for a new job, keep the following mental treatments in mind:

- "I am the answer to their calling."
- "A grand position is opening for me right now."

- "It is right for me to be employed profitably."
- "I am perfect for the job." Claim that it is yours now. Do not project this wish into the future. It is a fact right now.

And most important, don't forget to balance your life between work and play!

"When you judge another, you do not define them, you define yourself."
—Wayne Dyer

Stop finding fault

In our daily mental work, we need to address all of our habits. Good or bad, we need to look at them honestly.

One of the things we do constantly is blame or accuse. Our work is to stop finding fault in others. When we do this "fault finding," we are giving power to negativity. We see others as incomplete. The errors of others are their problems, and it is none of our business. We shouldn't concern ourselves with others' mistakes.

If someone asks your opinion, be helpful, thoughtful, and constructive, but not critical or hurtful. Remember the other is also in a state of unfoldment relative to his or her understanding. Your duty is to be kind and supportive.

"Finding Fault is finding trouble."
—*William W. Walter*

"...because you can!"

The way you speak to yourself internally causes your world to change

An unsuccessful or poor business is like a sickness. You can heal it the same way. So your mental work consists of understanding how to heal the business' ailing condition.

When experiencing business trouble, it is not enough to research new methods and techniques or develop new markets, products, or services.

Although you can consult the many helpful resources available today, you also need to take the time to think about the true reasons why your business is lacking customers or failing in general.

Poor business has its origin in the mentality, and that's where it needs to be corrected. Don't blame it on any outside circumstances. Know that it is you who created your business, good or bad.

My neighbor recently shared this anecdote regarding a restaurant he used to frequent:

Frank's story

"There is a sushi restaurant I avoid these days because the owner always steps over and starts in on how bad business is or how slow yesterday was or do I think everyone is suffering because of the economy or weather or summer vacation schedules. His lack of mental work awareness is costing him customers!"

Yes, my neighbor is absolutely right. The business owner's belief that the economy, weather, or anything outside of his sense is making his business slow or bad is a mistake. He exaggerates this sense by talking to his customers about the problems he encounters. He therefore makes it even worse in his own mind and alienates his already waning customers. What a tragedy!

You must apply what you have learned so far. You are in the process of finding out who and what you are and are working mentally to improve your daily experience. Remember that you are the thinker, and you are the cause.

Listen to your internal dialogue and make sure that all of your conversations with yourself are positive and full of hopeful anticipations. Know that all work starts in the mental, and all work continues there forever.

"There is no end to education. It is not that you read a book, pass an examination, and finish with education. The whole of life, from the moment you are born to the moment you die, is a process of learning."
—*Jiddu Krishnamurti*

Always work for the highest possible goal

Expect only the best in everything you do, and don't lower your standard. With humble gratitude and appreciation, it should never be a struggle to achieve any desired position. You just have to go for

"...because you can!"

it, persevere, keep hope and expectation alive, and create what you want.

If you can use your intelligence and wisdom to live a happier life, you can also live a more successful life. Your work is to claim that wealth and happiness is yours, and feel it.

You cannot say "My business is good" and then act the opposite by complaining to others that it has been slow all day. You stifle yourself and your business by thinking that the location is not good enough, you are in the wrong season, or any other negative thought.

Business is as good as you think it is. Reverse those negative, fearful thoughts and know that there are plenty of customers wanting your services; they are seeking your goods. You have goods or provide a service others desire, and you are committed to high-quality assistance.

Intelligence, our almighty source, fulfills all needs and therefore will send you customers. It will provide you with a job or abundance in many other forms.

What a feeling of freedom!

You are a perfect particle of mind, the substance of the Universe. Never think you are in need. Never see yourself as wanting. You desire, you create, and your dream is yours.

Mental Work

Know that you and your business are the response to someone's desire and vice versa. There are unlimited goods and enough for everyone in this Universe. Business is the activity of bringing the affluence of the Universe to this visible dimension.

Remember the Law of Least Effort: no resistance means that you don't have to work so hard. Rather, love your job, your work, your calling, and create a positive frequency.

Play and enjoy, and be creative while doing what you chose as your vocation. With this demeanor, your work will become an effortless enjoyment.

"Everything in the universe has a purpose. Indeed, the invisible intelligence that flows through everything in a purposeful fashion is also flowing through you."
—Wayne Dyer

Work on your connection to the Universe

Our work is to acknowledge the Godhood in everyone and the Oneness of all souls. Our Consciousness is what connects us to the source of all Being.

The harmony or discords of our lives depend upon our views of every circumstance. We all have our own viewpoints, but we need to bring them into accordance with Universal Laws.

"...because you can!"

The goal of Perfection is the Ultimate. We are striving to reach that goal.

Since no one is made alike and we are in different stages of unfoldment at all times, each of us pursues this goal differently. We accomplish this journey relative to the understanding we have acquired at this time.

Now you should realize that none of our problems are alike due to the different sense we all maintain. However, we are headed in the same direction, upward and onward, each of us in its proper time. We are on our own path, guided by our daily choices.

There is no need to rush or worry. Eventually we'll reach the destination of eternal bliss and Universal harmony, but only when we sincerely strive for this state of being.

**"Every person is a God in embryo.
Its only desire is to be born."
—Deepak Chopra**

Everything we do is created in our minds first. Your correct mental work is your savior.

Stop being too busy for the right things in life...because you can!

ANSWER THESE QUESTIONS HONESTLY:

1. Why is mental work so important?
2. Does your body have sensation of its own? Can your body "know" anything?
3. Do you like what you see when you look in the mirror?
4. Is your work schedule hectic? Can you change it?
5. Do you feel you never have the time for the things you want to do?
6. Do you like your job, or do you want to change to a vocation you love?
7. How is the quality of your work? Does it need improvement?
8. Can you maintain your thoughts of the highest quality you can sense?
9. What is the ultimate goal for everyone?
10. Can you see that everything is created in mind first? Explain.

CHAPTER 10

ABUNDANCE

"It is your right to be rich. You are here to lead the abundant life, to be happy, radiant and free. You should, therefore, have all the money you need to lead a full, happy, prosperous life."
—*Dr. Joseph Murphy*

Poverty is not a virtue

You are born to live in comfort. You live in an abundant world, and it is perfectly alright to be wealthy. These are strong statements and, looking at the world today and those who suffer from poverty or experience their incomes dwindling, it surely seems presumptuous; nevertheless, it is the truth.

Working from a Universal Law standpoint, however, it is your birthright to live in abundance, and it is perfectly fine to be rich, as long as you use your wealth wisely and correctly.

"...because you can!"

We all have a different sense of what wealth means. How much wealth do you need to be rich? You might think it takes millions to call yourself rich. Your neighbor might think living comfortably without having to worry about money to pay the bills equals wealth. I, on the other hand, might think of riches in a purely mental way.

> **"All riches have their origin in mind. Wealth is in ideas—not money."**
> *—Robert Collier*

Most people think of abundance as money, which is a mistake. Money is only a convenient means of exchange and nothing more. In the old days, items like salt, pepper, tea, gold, and silver were used. It's not about your means of payment for getting the things you want. It's what the value of the desired objects or comforts represent to you.

Who cares if you get your car handed down from your parents, your house as an inheritance, a new sweater (that you've eyeballed for a while now) as a birthday gift? Isn't it all money in usable form?

> **"Wealth flows from energy and ideas."**
> *—William Feather*

You circulate money

Supply, your money, does not come from a paycheck or any other outside source, even though it

Abundance

looks that way. This visible paycheck is only a symbol of your ability to produce wealth.

You don't spend your money—you circulate it. You exchange it for things you want or think you need. You exchange dollars for useful items such as gas, groceries, rent, and clothing, for example, which all in turn keep the economy strong on a more Universal level.

Always keep the sense of circulating instead of spending. Thinking of the flow of money as a circle makes it come back to you. However, "spending it" would mean losing it in the worldly sense. In reality, you can't lose anything. You only exchange money for things you need or want.

"Money is always there but the pockets change; it is not in the same pockets after a change, and that is all there is to say about money."
—*Gertrude Stein*

You will always get something for your money, even though it might be an experience rather than an item. For example, a vacation will provide the needed rest, or going to the museum will educate or inform you, and so on.

On the other hand, negatively speaking, let's say you are gambling away your money. Of course you think you've lost it. Well, you didn't lose it. You received a temporary feeling of excitement and entertainment value in return, even though the outcome was not to your liking.

"...because you can!"

Think about these things!

"When I chased after money, I never had enough. When I got my life on purpose and focused on giving of myself and everything that arrived into my life, then I was prosperous."
—*Wayne Dyer*

What is income?

Income, although it looks like it's coming from your line of work or paycheck, is really "out go."

Money doesn't come from outside of you. It is compensation coming in from your "out go" or "out flow" of services provided: your creativity, your talents, and your services rendered or your thoughts of plenty and abundant ideas manifested.

Feel it. Know it. You are wealth!

In order to create income, you need a strong determination and aim for your goals. You have to be focused and not double-minded, muddled, procrastinating, or indecisive.

For example, I've been drawn to reading metaphysical books more and more for years. Every day I spend hours thinking about mind and the Laws of the Universe and how they work. As with everything, there is a reason for my actions and desire.

When I listen to myself carefully, it feels right and it makes me feel good. Time flies when I'm absorbed in reading and studying. I have a sense of satisfaction. I am uplifted, content, happy, and full of purpose. These pleasant feelings were in fact signals, and they were showing me the way. These clues and instincts guided me to my purpose long before I picked up the pencil and began to write.

Being on the right path, no matter what your occupation (teacher, nurse, firefighter, gardener, salesperson, and so on) will be rewarding and will lift your sense of life to a new dimension. It will inspire you and make you feel fulfilled, catapulting you to a higher frequency.

So ask yourself: How do I feel about my field of expertise? Did I choose the right vocation? Do I want to continue on this path? What is my purpose or calling?

The clearer your purpose and the more focused your work, the better your income will "appear." It will be in exact proportion to your self-confidence, self-worth, and your accomplishments.

Remember, all things you receive, including gifts, unexpected monies, inheritance, and surprise winnings, are income and part of your abundance.

"Success is not the key to happiness. Happiness is the key to success. If you love what you are doing, you will be successful."
—*Albert Schweitzer*

"...because you can!"

Be careful what you wish for

As with all desires, when thought is applied correctly pertaining to abundance, it is so powerful that it can manifest anything. So watch what you think, because it will also manifest your wrong thoughts or mistaken sense. It can also cause poverty and scarceness.

The Law of Cause and Effect, or Like attracts Like, does not differentiate; it only produces. It is no respecter of persons. You are the cause of all that befalls you every day of your life. Take that responsibility, and be careful what you wish for!

"Only one who devotes himself to a cause with his whole strength and soul can be a true master. For this reason mastery demands all of a person."
—*Albert Einstein*

Be specific in your desire or wish. After you have outlined the desire in detail, bring it to a solid conclusion. Think it, feel it, and claim it. Feeling (or love) is key and necessary to produce all manifestations as discussed in previous chapters.

Watch the doubt as it is always a deterrent and will stifle your progress. When you are wishy-washy, your results will be half way.

Keep your desires good and fair. Your goals should be good for all concerned and for your own good, clean enjoyment. Be confident and act good. Think good, be good—or like God.

Remember that success is natural!

"You pray in your distress and in your need; would that you might also pray in the fullness of your joy and in your days of abundance."
—Khalil Gibran

Work with the laws, not against them

All Universal Laws are facts. They are unshakable, constant, and forever; they are responsive as to cause and effect, and always will be.

The Law of Like attracts Like and the Law of Cause and Effect are always in action, so think abundant thoughts and see yourself wealthy in all aspects (not just in receiving money) because you are the maker of everything.

Lift your sense from where you are now, and see where you want to be. Start changing your sense of limitations and practice step by step to see yourself in a more abundant light. There is no reason you should not, or cannot, be wealthy. Self-doubt and your own thoughts of limitations will put you in a scarce situation.

Cease your thoughts of limitations and you will find yourself increasingly abundant in exact proportion to your belief. Hopefully, later in the study and through your grasp of this science, you will learn to keep up this level of having plenty. All of your learning and daily practice culminates eventually and ultimately into Understanding, which in turn will provide for you.

"...because you can!"

Know that all is NOW, and do not put it in the future. Your light shines at this very moment.

> **"Visualize this thing that you want, see it, feel it, believe in it. Make your mental blue print, and begin to build."**
> *—Robert Collier*

What is the most important thing to you right now?

Make a list of your wishes and dreams, and review it often. It might not be money. Stay focused. Start to analyze, systematize, and reason about your aspirations. Claim your wants and then release them to the Universe. Know that it is already done, and know that it is good and the Law will take care of it. It works the same for all of your desires.

You are success NOW. As you have learned, feeling or the mother element does the producing, so feel it, and feel it, and feel it again. There is plenty of everything in the Universe for everyone, enough abundance for all. Look around you; it cannot be depleted. The Universe, Nature, will reproduce more and more of itself for you to enjoy.

> **"After a certain point, money is meaningless. It ceases to be the goal. The game is what counts."**
> *—Aristotle Onassis*

Yes, the enjoyment is what counts. Therefore, money should be used wisely and constructively.

Wealth, as I pointed out earlier, is a state of consciousness or state of mind. You are here to live a balanced life, not one of opulence and excess. Your life should be a rich life, full of beauty and comfort.

We all have a different sense of wealth. There is a reason why poor people are poor, and there is a reason why rich people are rich. Poor people feel scarce and lacking of, even in their basic needs. Sadly enough, they believe that it's the way it is for them and see no way out.

Wealthy people feel entitled to be rich. They expect wealth, comfort, luxury, and they surround themselves with beautiful things. Only the best is good enough. They have what we call Wealth-Consciousness.

People that gain wealth are usually the ones that do what they love. They stay focused and they are persistent, and they know what they want out of life and their jobs or careers.

They usually invest their money into their own venture and not into someone else's company or project. They are unrelenting in the pursuit of their goals.

They educate themselves and gain much knowledge and experience trying to be the best they can be in their field and do not waste time worrying about failure or doubting their abilities and instincts. They know they "can." They see the end result ever moving in the direction of their goals.

Remember, you can, too!

> **"Not what we have but what we enjoy constitutes our abundance."**
> **—*Epicurus***

You can have the same because we are all of the same substance, same capabilities, and same Universal fabric. You *are* Wealth. You are a wealth of knowledge, talent, abilities, love, and capacity to give to mankind. You are useful, loving, giving, and generous. Imagine yourself wealthy in all aspects. Feel it. This is a command!

Imagine the good you can do with your newfound wealth. Use it wisely and generously. Inner actions always precede outer action, so believe that you have it NOW, and it shall come to pass.

> **"Shallow men believe in luck. Strong men believe in cause and effect."**
> **—*Ralph Waldo Emerson***

How to think abundantly

Dollars are the outcome of your honest and accurate thinking. Value yourself and keep your sense about yourself high. Feel good about yourself. Let go of that guilt trip or shame. Let go of that sense of inferiority, and feel secure within yourself.

Nothing is impossible to demonstrate with self-confidence and courage. Know that you are important, yet be humble and grateful. Feel powerful, yet retain a sincere desire of wanting to provide service to humankind. Always see the value in YOU—that is what attracts money!

> **"Weakness of attitude becomes weakness of character."**
> **—*Albert Einstein***

Start with practicing "thought modifications"

Observe your thoughts, analyze them, and improve them by thinking and feeling more abundant thoughts. "My sales are increasing every day," "I can pay my bills easily and comfortably," and "I have plenty of everything I need" are good starting affirmations.

Negative thoughts like "I'm broke" or "I don't have enough" are no longer acceptable.

When you apply your new attitude, your sense of riches will improve a little bit at a time. The increased dollars in your account will prove to you that you are on the right path.

> **"What you bless you multiply, what you condemn you lose."**
> **—*Dr. Joseph Murphy***

The quote above means you have to love being wealthy and abundantly supplied. Most of all bless or appreciate your riches. You have to truly be grateful for everything, even the smallest things in life, and it will multiply. In your prayer, wish goodness, happiness, and abundance for every human being.

Warning: If you are not grateful or take your blessings for granted, they will be lost.

It is your choice. You are free to choose and think anything you so desire. So choose wisely!

Let Divine Wisdom guide you. Infinite Intelligence watches over you and governs you all of the time. Trust and know that everything is already finished in the absolute state, but here in this relative state we must awaken to this fact. We have to remember who we truly are. We must recall what we have forgotten—namely, that all is already good.

"The will to win, the desire to succeed, the urge to reach your full potential...these are the keys that will unlock the door to personal excellence."
—*Confucius*

You are the source of your riches

You are the source of your riches—not someone else or something outside of you such as your job, your parents, or your spouse. As I stressed before, it does not depend on the economy or outside circumstances. It depends solely on your attitude, beliefs, and wealth consciousness.

When you've learned how to create, you will be the master of your life. Creation works the same way for everything, not just for money. Your whole life depends on your understanding of this innate power of creation.

Abundance

Wealth starts in your mind. Your true riches spring from your own ideas. You have Imagination, and Imagination is the creative power of the Universe. Visualize all you desire and claim success. State often "Money is circulating freely, and I am economically healthy" and "I am a channel of the Universe through which abundance is expressed."

"Happiness is not something ready made. It comes from your own actions."
—Dalai Lama

Money doesn't make your life perfect

Having money makes some aspects of your life easier: paying your bills, sending your kids to a good school, or living in a beautiful home. However, if you are stricken by some incurable disease, wouldn't you want to heal the disease first? Of course, you say. It stands to reason.

So why don't you start today and change your lifestyle to a more healthy mental environment. I'm not talking about the obvious like drugs, excess drinking, and so on. I'm talking about healthy thoughts of "I am well," "I am a perfect mental being," "I am life, and I feel good," and "I have everything I need."

A better basic lifestyle and affirmative thought pattern will set the foundation for a more harmonious state of mind. It will set the stage for you to allow wealth consciousness to flow easier through you. You will have a better sense of yourself, of feeling healthy

"...because you can!"

and happy, so it will be natural to take the next step to a more financially abundant life.

See the connection? You start with simpler improvements, and you work your way up the ladder of happiness!

"The first wealth is health."
—*Ralph Waldo Emerson*

Ask yourself, "Does money make me feel secure?" Where does the sense of security come from? It comes from the inner knowing that you are self-sufficient and creative. It comes from the conviction that you are all powerful. Security derives from valuing your true self.

Ask yourself, "What will more money do for me and what would I do with it?"

Contemplate those questions and make a list.

Ask yourself, "How can I be of service to humankind, and how can I contribute more?"

It is a giving and taking, a two-way street, as I will remind you throughout this book. This is an all-inclusive Universe. No one should be forgotten, and no one should suffer.

We are all beings of Light. We are all in this together. We are One.

"Just as treasures are uncovered from the earth, so virtue appears from good deeds, and wisdom

appears from a pure and peaceful mind. To walk safely through the maze of human life, one needs the light of wisdom and the guidance of virtue."
—Buddha

What is your sense of quality?

Your sense of quality shapes your environment. Quality trumps quantity, as we know. Surround yourself with lovely, beautiful things and good quality people. It's better to have a few good friends than a lot of acquaintances; seek quality rather than quantity.

By being of high quality yourself, you will draw people with like character into your world. Honesty, integrity, and respect are high-quality virtues and necessary for a successful, long lasting business as well as healthy relationships.

Quick money scams and getting something for nothing are not the way to lasting wealth. Lottery winners have proven "easy come, easy go" by demonstrating that as much as 90 percent of winners lose their money within three to five years. Their sense of wealth is not established at the time of winning, and they have not mentally earned their money. Within no time, most of them are back to where they started.

Looking at it from a mental standpoint, being wealthy is not always the best situation for you. (I can see you shaking your head, saying it would be just fine for you...ha!) It can deter you from finding your true self, and binds you to a world of materialism.

"...because you can!"

For some people, too much money can also be a burden and add unwanted responsibility. Many people experience the agony of not knowing who their true friends are after finding wealth. You also have to have the know-how of managing money properly and wisely. You must have the skills.

A slight reminder from the Mental House Cleaning chapter: don't be attached to stuff. The obsession for more is a trap. It is a toxic message we receive daily from the commercialization of the world around us. However, more often leads to clutter—physically and spiritually.

More is not always better. Discern the difference between enjoying your stuff and being attached to your stuff. You have already done your housekeeping. Why start all over again?

The only stuff you really need is a True Sense of Love and the Understanding of the Laws of Life and the application thereof. Nothing more, nothing less.

Why? Because when you have gained this true sense of what Love really is and understand the Laws of Life, everything you'll ever need will be added onto you automatically. You will have found heaven.

"Love and compassion are necessities, not luxuries. Without them humanity cannot survive."
—*Dalai Lama*

However, people with a wealth consciousness, even if they lose everything, will gain it back within a short period of time, due to their sense of wealth. Donald Trump is a perfect example, as I am sure everyone knows.

We send out vibrations constantly. Make sure that you are sending out thoughts of plenty. Believe in your prosperity, even if you have to start with little because it will multiply according to your sense. Keep your feeling on the right side, and know that you deserve it.

"Doing what you love is the cornerstone of having abundance in your life."
—Wayne Dyer

You and Abundance, up close and personal

You are a valuable person and you have to value your family and friends. You also have to value your bosses, your co-workers, and your business partners and, most of all, your clients. It is imperative that you give the best service to your clients.

If you are willing to do whatever it takes—doing a good job for your employer and doing it happily, lovingly, and joyously—you are winning the game.

Your commitment to learn all about your job and keep abreast of new technology or any other know-how's necessary to be a valuable employee will give you confidence.

Keep in mind that for your excellent services, you will be compensated plentifully. You now know that you deserve good compensation, benefits, and all that the company offers.

If you are self-employed, you know that clients are seeking your services and that there are enough clients for everyone. Since your business is a mental business operated through the thoughts and feelings of the owner (you), the Law of Attraction will provide plenty of business.

Surround yourself with other successful people, just as you surround yourself with good and loving people. Again, Like attracts Like and those like-minded people will flock to you, and new doors will open every day.

Now, remember that even though you know your worth and expect the best, you are also immensely appreciative for the abundance you receive.

"In our natural state, we are glorious beings. In the world of illusion, we are lost and imprisoned, slaves to our appetites and our will to false power."
—*Marianne Williamson*

Saving money

It has been said in the Metaphysical community that saving money is a demonstration of distrust in your mental capabilities of being able to create more at any time. I do not agree with this viewpoint as I think saving money is necessary for several reasons.

Abundance

To put the dollars in the bank instead of spending them indiscriminately and wasting them on whims and material goods shows strength of character. Having an emergency fund will give you a feeling of "having," and you will sleep better not worrying so much. A sense of security and independence will strengthen your ability to buy and enjoy things you do want.

Hoarding money when you could do good things with it, for yourself and others, is miserly, but saving and investing money to establish a healthy bank account is intelligence at work.

"Nothing is more important than reconnecting with your bliss. Nothing is as rich. Nothing is more real."
—*Deepak Chopra*

Be prosperous…because you can!

ANSWER THESE QUESTIONS HONESTLY:

1. What does abundance mean to you?
2. If you could have anything you want, what would you wish for?
3. Did you choose the right vocation? Are you compensated plentifully?
4. What do you think is your calling?
5. What is the most important thing to you right now?
6. Does money make you feel secure?
7. What would you do with money if you could get a lot of it?
8. What is your sense of quality?
9. Do you enjoy the money you have? Do you use it wisely?
10. Are you economically healthy? Can you improve your current status?

CHAPTER 11

RELATIONSHIPS

"Where there is love there is life."
—Mohandas Gandhi

The only true relationship you can ever have is with yourself

When I think about my relationship with myself, what comes to mind?

I must admit, the more thought I give this question, the more I realize that I have a great relationship with myself. I don't annoy myself; I don't ignore myself; I enjoy myself when alone; I take care of myself; and, most of all, I like myself.

I can keep myself busy easily. I'm never bored, and I spend lots of quiet time in reflection. I like to improve myself, educate, and treat myself well.

"...because you can!"

It doesn't take much to do all of the above, and it doesn't take money or a lot of time.

How do you find quietness in a busy day, you ask? Yes, I have a full-time job between my work at the museum and my writing/teaching program. But to me it's as natural as breathing. I have trained myself to think that way. I work it into my daily schedule easily.

It's all about your priorities. Instead of going to the mall, I read a book. Instead of going to the beauty parlor, I work on my goal list...you get the point.

I focus on myself without being egocentric. I enjoy without grandeur. I take care by allowing myself plenty of rest, and I keep busy by practicing right thinking and studying. I always put myself first without being selfish.

Everything I do is focused on the mental, not physical, process.

> **"Spiritual relationship is far more precious than physical. Physical relationship divorced from spiritual is body without soul."**
> **—Mohandas Gandhi**

Who do I think I am?

I have always wondered who I am and why I am the way I am.

Many of us ask that question at some point in our lives. We must realize that we have been, at least in our younger years, shaped by parents and family, community, religion, ethnicity, and education.

Yet as we mature, we often divert from those influences that had seemingly made a lasting impression. We all decided to make unique life choices and start drawing our own conclusions that may indeed vary from how we were raised; even so, we keep many of the old beliefs. This certainly shows in the experiences we now encounter.

This is what I've learned:

What I am is a mental being, looking for my purpose as I unfold the inherent intelligence within me. And if, as I am certain, the purpose of my life is to enjoy myself, then I am on the right path. I am consciously trying to accomplish this daily.

What I am is a unique instrument born of the Universe, expressing life and serving my purpose by contributing to the Allness of Good.

In reality this process is already accomplished. The Allness of Good is already all there is. What I mean by this is that the Universe is made out of goodness and, therefore, we do not have to add to it or interfere. However, we have to find and acknowledge and then externalize what is already positive within us.

"Glorify who you are today, do not condemn who you were yesterday, and dream of who you can be tomorrow."
—Neale Donald Walsch

"...because you can!"

So how is your relationship with *yourself*?

Do you like yourself? Do you spend time with yourself? Do you have alone time, and how do you handle those quiet moments? Do you escape into activities to avoid yourself? Do you struggle with feelings of loneliness the minute you are alone? Are there times you really want to be alone but fear hurting someone else's feelings?

Do you treat yourself well? Are you taking care of yourself physically and mentally?

Do you acknowledge your Godhood?

In your daily mantra, say to yourself, "I am all there is in my world" and live accordingly. Realizing that your world consists of your perception of "your world" will bring a different perspective to your life experience.

The realization of your importance, in an unselfish way, will make you a better person. It will give you the strength to move on gracefully and enable you to take care of your immediate environment. This new-found empowerment will ripple out, affecting everyone with whom you come into contact.

"To enjoy good health, to bring true happiness to one's family, to bring peace to all, one must first discipline and control one's own mind. If a man can control his mind he can find the way to Enlightenment, and all wisdom and virtue will naturally come to him."
—Buddha

Your true family

Your true family consists of the people that share your life with you on a similar frequency. They are the ones you can depend on, trust, have fun with, enjoy their company, and want to spend time with. These people are not always your family by birth.

You will encounter them in different stages of your life. They will enter your world when you need them. They will be with you through thick and thin. They will grow with you, but most of all they will respect your individuality.

As we know, we don't get to choose our birth family members. Sometimes we are born into a family that seems to be different, one that does not fit into our perception of who we are. Such differences may, in fact, enlarge over time as some members cling to the past and others fear the present, while others try to control some point in the future.

I know many families that have great love for each other. But there are many that barely speak to each other and have nothing in common. Families are a complex subject as they involve many different people and personalities—each of them making their own life choices. However, no matter what the situation, we choose our relationships.

"The bond that links your true family is not one of blood, but of respect and joy in each other's life."
—Richard Bach

"...because you can!"

Ilene's story

"I was born into a large family—six kids in all. We were taught, as a brood, to love, protect and help each other with all our daily needs. This is a wonderful premise from which to work from as a child; however, the dynamics of the family changed substantially as we grew up, formed our own opinions about how to live our lives, and dealt with the challenges of life in general.

Some of us developed addictions to drugs and alcohol, some to shopping and food. Each made their own choices—for better or for worse.

Being the middle child, I've always been the "fixer," the caretaker, the conduit who constantly tried to make everything and everyone "better." This is what I learned as a child coming from poor background, watching what was going on—you never give up when someone needs your help.

While this is an ideal motto to live by, I have learned through the years and through studying the core principles of Metaphysics and several philosophies that this kind of logic is no respecter of Individuality.

I could spend my whole life trying to make everyone else's lives better but at what cost? Where is my life in all this? What is my purpose for doing this? Is it really to help them, or to avoid dealing with my own life?

Relationships

I had to ask myself some very serious questions about motive. I had to get real about who I was and what I was doing.

When the light of my mentality finally came on, I recognized a few things. First off, my siblings are all complete and whole within themselves. They made their own decisions, right or wrong, and I cannot control that. I can give them some tools to help them make better choices, but I cannot live their lives for them. I needed to respect them as individuals in their own right.

Secondly, my primary concern always needs to be ME. Not me in a personal sense, but ME as an intelligent, complete individual in my own right. My thinking needs to be right about myself and who I am—why I'm here—before I can be of any use to anyone else.

And lastly, I can control no one or any situation but my own. In letting go of this childhood belief, I was free to live as an intelligent adult.

"You don't choose your family. They are God's gift to you, as you are to them."
—*Desmond Tutu*

Families and relationships are sometimes complicated—layered and convoluted with personal sense, emotional residue, and no clear lines of respect drawn between each other. Yet, it is truly very uncomplicated if we remove all "personal" sense and really respect the Law of Individuality.

When I need a wake up call, I head to a mirror and look right in it. That's who I need to deal with—here and now. My family portrait is contained in that one image."

"You have to grow from the inside out. None can teach you, none can make you spiritual. There is no other teacher but your own soul."
—*Swami Vivekananda*

The family environment

In a family environment, the issues are mostly related individuals' interactions. Certain members are dependent on a brother or sister, someone they feel is stronger, and others are just the opposite. They try to control the seemingly weaker ones.

Some family members are always involved in everyone's business, critical of what they do and judgmental as to how they should live their lives. Some, on the other hand, are always there for you. They are dependable and supportive. Some are enabling, thinking that their help can fix you or your problems.

Then, there are family gatherings that you would rather not attend, but you don't want to deal with the ensuing guilt trip. The pressures of certain members wanting to control how the holidays are spent or a wedding is planned are part of the stressful family business that you'd rather stay out of...

Relationships

Find a balance in your dealings with your family. Be helpful, but not stifling. Be supportive, but not demanding. Be loving toward them, but not overbearing.

Live and let live!

"If you love someone, set them free. If they come back they're yours; if they don't they never were."
—*Richard Bach*

Marriage

Oh, this personal sense of marriage!

Everyone sees marriage as a companionship here on earth. It includes having children, making a home together, earning a living, and of course having legal advantages. It should be a "marriage made in heaven."

But even the so-called physical act of marriage is only an opportunity to learn, grow, and unfold. Loving companionship is a blessing and should be cherished, but is not necessary in this state of being. A companion is a helpmate, not a need.

Unfortunately, the dynamic of many partnerships is one of dependency. You are an individual, so don't become dependent. There is a lot to learn from each other, but dependency is not part of it.

If you cling on to the other or act needy, he or she will be resentful and feel smothered. The same issues occur when one wants to control the other. Marriage should not be a power struggle; you are equal partners in life.

Sadly enough, we make our relationship with our mates the most personal of relationships. "Of course," you say, "he [or she] is the closest person I know. I share my life with him [or her]." Yes, but your partner is still an individual and the Law of Individuality demands that each of you live your own life.

We easily forgive family and friends for their mistakes and behavior, but when it comes to our mates we are much more sensitive and opinionated. A fifty percent divorce rate is proof of that. Rather than resisting and controlling every situation, it is much easier to allow others, including your partner, to do as they please.

We all have the right to think and make choices of our own liking. How wonderful!

"Being deeply loved by someone gives you strength, while loving someone deeply gives you courage."
—Lao Tzu

Frankly speaking, your mate does not owe you anything but *respect*.

Since the most vital relationship is the one with yourself, you should nurture or develop this inner relationship, even when you are married or in a committed relationship with someone.

Separate interests and activities can be shared at the end of the day. Quiet time, stillness, and meditation should be part of your personal agenda. This personal space time will keep you sane and balanced.

I know a lot of men and women who are content to be at home, relaxing, reading or engaging in their own hobbies, while their partners flit from one function to the other. Each handles his or her time differently, benefitting at the end of the day from the happiness of the other.

"When marrying, ask yourself this question: Do you believe that you will be able to converse well with this person into your old age? Everything else in marriage is transitory."
—*Friedrich Nietzsche*

What does marriage represent in the mental?

The concept of marriage in the mental represents the blending together of the female and male elements in mind. This is not a physical action, but a mental one.

It takes the male and the female elements, knowing and feeling, to create anything. What is made or appears in the visible world was conceived in the mental, nurtured by good thought and born through the conviction or understanding of your consciousness.

The birth of a child is the visible expression of this mental process. The visible symbol of earthly marriage is the coming together of a man and woman to create more life. We are all composed of the male and female elements. We are a complete whole, and we give birth to more wholeness. We are multiplying life into its visible form.

The focal point of our journey is to unfold and gain an understanding of the truth of life and how the creation or birth process works. All else will fall into place naturally.

We also learn from the characteristics of our mates. Our partner mirrors back our good and bad qualities alike. If you don't like your partner's action or attitude, change your sense about him or her and he or she will change according to your sense.

Therefore, a true and equal partnership with loving, understanding, and support of each other is mostly desirable. It is the ideal, and it can be realized.

"You don't develop courage by being happy in your relationships everyday. You develop it by surviving difficult times and challenging adversity."
—*Epicurus*

Your children

We do not own anyone, not even our children. Your children are not your property; they are born through you but not of you.

You are an instrument supporting the urge of the multiplication of life. You are a vehicle enabling life to express more of life through you.

Each newborn baby is born an individual, perfect and good. You as the parent are responsible to guide and care for the child for a period of time, making sure the basic needs are met for his or her survival. You love your children and teach them to be good people, but the time will come for you to let go.

"Your children are not your children. They are the sons and daughters of Life's longing for itself. They came through you but not from you and though they are with you yet they belong not to you."
—*Khalil Gibran*

Your biggest accomplishments are the values you instill in your children. Children need the freedom to choose for themselves. Yes, you need to set boundaries and give them rules, but do not stifle them. Make them self-sufficient, and teach them to honor their elders. This is the principle thing.

Sadly enough, there is a terrible drug epidemic in this country among young people, too much of letting them drift, too few rules, no curfews, no respect, and too much money available are just some of the culprits. Parents are working many hours and not spending quality time with their kids. Parents, drug and alcohol abusers themselves, are not able to cope with how they see the world.

"...because you can!"

All this is correctable and is only a manifestation of an unsatisfied, immature mind. Children have to grow and learn their lessons, and they have to test and learn by their challenges just as we adults do. Still immature, they need guidance and love, but they also need freedom.

> **"Real magic in relationships means an absence of judgment of others."**
> —*Wayne Dyer*

Live by example

Children will notice your honesty, your good character, and your sincerity. They will model their parents, even though they would never admit to it. I know it looks differently in their teenage years. They are struggling to find their identity amid a world of peer pressure, and they can be quite defiant. Teens challenge. They push back.

However, you, with your love and care, will get through those periods. But you need to be present with them. Listen to them. Acknowledge them. Love them. Make them know you are always there for them. Stick with it, and keep walking the talk.

I personally love their teenage years. What an amazing and joyful time! Watching your children turning into men and women is absolutely fascinating. You can observe as individuality starts to express itself. Yes, sometimes by several nose rings, tattoos, and flaming orange hair, but it's okay that they experiment. We did, didn't we?

If you don't press too hard, they will grow out of this stage. They are trying to find themselves, not yet in a mature way. They will rebel if you force or try to control them, but their newfound self is only trying to establish it's natural SELF.

Having a son myself, I remember him as a teen looking at me sometimes with disbelief, rolling his eyes at my teachings. But as he grew up, I never pushed any of my convictions and beliefs on him, and he developed a good character. I just taught him to be honest, sincere, and a good member of society.

He is open to social differences even though he is strongly opinionated, and he lets people live the way they see fit. His contribution to the world meant standing up for his country, and so he went to fight in the Iraq war.

I wish for no one to feel the agony of having their sons and daughters join the relentless insanity of war, but I honor their courage, commitment, and pride in their country. Needless to say, I am very proud of him!

> **"Love... it surrounds every being and extends slowly to embrace all that shall be."**
> —*Khalil Gibran*

"...because you can!"

Your friends

Since childhood you have picked your best friends, and during our lifetime you have chosen more. But you've also outgrown many of those relationships. If you have even one lifelong friend, you are blessed.

As your frequency changes, so will your friends and associates—yes, even your family. Sometimes they go away for a period of time and then reappear later in life. Sometimes you will never see them again. It is all a perfect dance, beautifully orchestrated by the Universe—Synchronicity at its best.

It is important that you surround yourself not just with beautiful and good things, but also with good and honest people that are on your mental frequency.

Choose the people in your environment very carefully. Make sure their character matches yours and their values are aligned with yours.

With this in mind, it is easy to appreciate the people around you, your family, and your friends. Be grateful that you have them and show them that you value each of them.

"Old friends pass away, new friends appear. It is just like the days. An old day passes, a new day arrives. The important thing is to make it meaningful: a meaningful friend—or a meaningful day."
—Dalai Lama

When you encounter a difficult period in your life, let no one see you hurt or angry. You can be firm and honest, but do not react to others in an unkind, confrontational way. Stay composed and reasonable, and stay away from personal opinions; and, most of all, mind your own business.

"It is never another person, condition, or thing that disturbs, angers, or hurts you. It is always your thought and feelings about what is said that disturbs angers or hurts you."
—*William W. Walter*

We all have plenty of work to do with our own business; there is no need to get involved in anyone else's!

Last but not least, don't mistake affection for Love. True love is all encompassing; affection is usually bestowed on a specific individual and lasts only for a certain time. Love lasts forever.

"Can miles truly separate you from friends...If you want to be with someone you love, aren't you already there?"
—*Richard Bach*

We always have expectancy from the other

Many times we have an expectancy of what others should be or what they would do. It is not your place to judge or tell others what to do. Take care of your own self, and correct your own wrong thinking;

"...because you can!"

I'm sure that should keep you busy for a while. I know it's keeping me occupied...

It is only your reaction to the other person that triggers a response in you that is either pleasant or disturbing. It is imperative to know that the other person speaks from his or her own viewpoint, not necessarily from the truth. So why do you care what the other person thinks about you?

If you are like-minded individuals, you will automatically attract each other. If you are not like-minded or on a similar frequency, let it go. We want to spend time with individuals who are on our wavelength, don't we?

> **"Love is always bestowed as a gift—freely, willingly and without expectation. We don't love to be loved; we love to love."**
> **—Leo Buscaglia**

How do we improve our relationships?

In your family life, take a look at your home and make it beautiful: plant flowers in the garden, burn some nice-smelling candles, or decorate your house with soft fabrics. Whatever you do, make it enjoyable. Think about what you and your family like; discover your style of living, and create more comfort. Men, mow that lawn or wash your partner's car without being asked!

Every aspect of your life touches someone else by rippling out toward your family, friends, and those you come into contact with. They will feel that the love you exude. Your immediate family living with you will appreciate the nurturing you are providing.

Find quality time to spend with your friends. Make memories together and know that the bond you create will last forever. Your casual relationships will benefit from your kindness and pleasantness. It's all good!

The good you experience comes from the good you give recognition to. It is what you see in yourself now. Watch your feelings toward people; it's a multiplier. You must start thinking of yourself as good and perfect. And you must think the same of others.

> **"Personal relationships are the fertile soil from which all advancement, all success, all achievement in real life grows."**
> *—Ben Stein*

What is true of me now?

Most of you will agree that your sense of yourself has to improve. Ask yourself, "What is true of me now?" Don't think of yourself as what you have been and the mistakes you've made. Keep it in the NOW. Who are you now?

Without condemnation, ask yourself, "What else do I need to improve? What thoughts and habits need changing?" However, don't see yourself as imperfect and in dire need of improvement as it will devalue you. See yourself as valuable.

"...because you can!"

What is true of you now may change your perspective on who remains with you now, what you do for a living now, what new interests you have now, and what new direction you are traveling in now. It brings everything into the NOW. Your answers will prompt new discoveries.

Finding out who you are now gives you the power to embrace or adjust.

"Do all things with love."
—*Og Mandino*

In the process of finding the value within yourself, you are only filling a lack of, or are improving, your sense of self. As you improve your sense of self, you heal the relationships with yourself and others.

You only have a sense of the "other," and we all have a different sense of *each* other. So it is important that your good sense of the other stays constant and does not waver.

Because we attract people that are on a similar frequency into our experience, this new and improved sense of yourself will bring better people into your life. Remember, Like attracts Like.

"Adopt the pace of nature: her secret is patience."
—*Ralph Waldo Emerson*

Patience

Patience, especially in relationships, is often thought of as putting up with something. Patience is more than endurance, such as enduring an unpleasant or annoying relationship.

Patience is the confidence of knowing that no matter what the appearance, all will work out in the big scheme of life.

Patience is Love. Do not mistake patience with accepting a wrong situation or abusive relationship. Do not put up with any situation in a relationship that is less than respectful or loving.

Most of all, respect yourself and love yourself, because, after all, you are the only one that has a true relationship with you.

> **"Have patience with all things, But,
> first of all with yourself."**
> —*Saint Francis de Sales*

Our relationship to the Universe and its creatures

Our love for the planet and its creatures, our good will to all, and our active desire to make things better will have a positive impact of great proportions on this earth.

Do not make the mistake of seeing the wrong, evil, or hardships around you and believing in their reality. Do not think you have to fight against it. All you have to do is to shut out all negative impressions and feelings from your thoughts, and carry on with your good work. Your world will respond. You will behold a perfect relationship with the Universe.

"...because you can!"

I have never understood how people cannot like animals, especially dogs, cats, and everyday household pets. It has been long proven that pets help bring peace and harmony to an individual. They are given to older people as companions and brought to visit children in hospitals to brighten their days. Service dogs are indispensable to so many people with physical disabilities.

I understand that maybe a spider or a snake might not be attractive to all (My friend doesn't like big, fat flies), but when you have looked into the eyes of any creature, surely you see Life and God, the connection to the Universe. How can you kill?

"Each blade of grass has its spot on earth whence it draws its life, its strength; and so is man rooted to the land from which he draws his faith together with his life."
—Joseph Conrad

Heal the violence

Studies show that the majority of domestic abuse is performed by butchers and law enforcement personnel.

This makes sense as both are in constant contact with violence and death. They lose all feeling for life. Butchers especially engage in killing "life" every day, so their sense of compassion for life has dwindled or does not exist. They warrant the violence with the "having to eat" excuse.

I do not call myself a vegetarian, but tend more and more to wean myself of meat derived by the killing of animals. We are taught to eat them; we say it's okay, but have you personally killed a cow, a pig, or a deer?

Law enforcement personnel constantly encounter dangerous criminals. They are heavily armed and are always on the defense. They are always in control and might feel the need to control their home lives the same way and, in the process, are hurting their loved ones. I am sure there are many loving, healthy families in this category that do not apply; but I am simply pointing out that certain job environments create a more volatile home situation.

My stepfather, rest his soul, was a World War II veteran and damaged goods, like so many Austrians and Germans that were forced to join the Nazi youth as mere children. His demeanor was hard and, even though he could be social and was a great neighbor, he had no problem killing the pigs or hens my mother raised. It was cruel in my eyes for him to raise the little piglets and then slaughter them with his bare hands. But not knowing better, he saw nothing wrong. His mind was disconnected from love, and he could not comprehend compassion. Sadly, it showed in the way he treated my mother.

"I object to violence because when it appears to do good, the good is only temporary; the evil it does is permanent."
—*Mohandas Gandhi*

"...because you can!"

All of Nature must be preserved. The oceans, forests, the mountains, the air, all species, and everything that we have received in such bounty must be cherished and honored.

We must be caretakers of what we have been given. We cannot ignore where this world is going. We cannot allow the destruction of the planet. We must stand up and walk with God's Love. It takes each person to make the whole, to fill the last piece of this puzzle.

"Peace cannot be achieved through violence; it can only be attained through understanding."
—*Ralph Waldo Emerson*

Walk with peace and love...because you can!

ANSWER THESE QUESTIONS HONESTLY:

1. How is your relationship with yourself? Do you love yourself?
2. Do you take care of yourself and treat yourself kindly?
3. Do you value and respect yourself?
4. Do you spend time with yourself?
5. Do you acknowledge your godhood?
6. What is true of you now? Has your sense of yourself improved?
7. Think about your relationship with your children. What can be improved?
8. Think about your relationship with your partner. What can be improved?
9. Do you know "who" you are right now? Make a list.
10. Are you patient? Give examples.

CHAPTER 12

THE TRUE MEANING OF LOVE

This is a message of love, not one of passion or infatuation, but true love—love for all humankind, all creatures, nature, the world, and, yes, the whole Universe. Love that sustains all, heals all, and conquers all pain and suffering.

We are One. We are connected, and the fabric of which we are made is Love.

"The moment you have in your heart this extraordinary thing called love and feel the depth, the delight, the ecstasy of it, you will discover that for you the world is transformed."
—Jiddu Krishnamurti

"...because you can!"

Why do we see so much hate and not Love?

All the hatred and destruction you see comes from a sense of inferiority. This includes envy from a lack of self-sufficiency, selfishness, frustration, thinking that you are powerless, as well as tremendous fear.

If people could find the power within themselves, they would stop hate and destruction, including self-destruction. They would know that they can have all the good there is without having to take from another. They would cease to long for others belongings and create riches for themselves, and they would cease to look for faults and weaknesses in those around them.

They would stop intolerance of other people, be it about ethnicity, social class, race, gender, or gender preference and/or religious views. They would stop the insanity of killing one another.

They would know that we are all made of the same substance, coming from the same source and, therefore, hate would be seen for what it is: wrong, evil, unnecessary, and pointless.

> **"Peace begins with a smile."**
> **—*Mother Teresa***

Start today!

Consider this: if we would start today, by just taking care of our family and friends, the spider effect would create world peace. Think about the social media today and envision the instantaneous and wide reach it has all over the world. It is clearly a visible symbol showing how we are all connected. If we can reach people anywhere on the planet by phone or e-mail, what do you think your mind and thoughts can do?

Your sense, your thought vibrations, and your feelings are connected to all life, whether you know it or not. It's that simple. And your contribution of good and well-intended pulsation is vital. Do not underestimate your power!

"Harmony is one phase of the law whose spiritual expression is love."
—James Allen

Go outdoors and look at nature around you. Even in the midst of a large city, you will find beauty if you just look deeply enough. Start loving what you see, no matter where you are.

I live in the center of Hollywood, Los Angeles, and from my desk looking through large, open French doors I can see my backyard. The many birds in the fountain outside my office window are chirping and playing in the water, returning my love by singing me a song and allowing me to get close to them.

The garden I enjoy and tend to, something that gives me so much pleasure, is giving back by flowering and glowing different shades of glorious colors. The vegetables I lovingly planted are rewarding my love by producing good crops for a delicious meal.

"...because you can!"

With doors wide open, I enjoy the breeze and feel the love that the Universe gives back to me, and every second I am thankful for being aware of those delightful moments.

Even as I am writing these words, the birds are singing in my garden and the warm California sun is brightening my day in this magical place I call home. How grateful I am! I wish that everyone on this plane could experience the same joy.

> **"Life without love is like a tree without blossoms or fruit."**
> —*Khalil Gibran*

Do you think you love enough?

Can you ever love enough? Do you love generously and spontaneously? Or do you expect something in return? Is your love an affection for a specific person or your children, or do you love everyone? Do you know the difference between true love, affection, infatuation, and liking someone?

Our answers will differ as we all have a unique sense of Love and what it means to us. What does Love mean to you?

> **"Let the beauty of what you love be what you do."**
> —*Rumi*

It all rests within you

You can be happy or sad, full of enthusiasm or discouragement; you can be strong or weak. You can love or hate, admire or envy. You can be full of joy and gratitude, or you can be miserable and spiteful. It is all up to you. It is your choice.

You can choose to think more and more of good qualities, and your mind will develop them in you, for you. Think strongly on courage, strength, and self-confidence. Expect good, peace, love, and joy, and feel them over and over again. Sleep with them, eat with them, walk with them, and be them. Do not allow any thought lesser than good enter your mind.

Most of all, learn to love and understand yourself first so that you will learn to love and understand everyone and all life.

> **"Love is life. And if you miss love, you miss life."**
> **—Leo Buscaglia**

Infatuation

Any time we think we love something or someone, we are looking through rose- colored glasses and overlook many otherwise unpleasant traits and behaviors. We shrug off the red flags that come up early in relationships because we want to believe that we've found our soul mate. We think we can adjust

"...because you can!"

to another's behavior and, many times, lose our own personality in the process. Conversely, we change, or we think we can change the other person.

When we truly love, we see only the good and perfect in the other and not their shortcomings. We are able to look beyond and find beauty in anything they do or say. We see the true spirit, the pure soul, and not the contaminated character.

The trouble is that in most early stages of relationships, we do not love; instead we have affection, emotions, and lust, but those are not lasting or enduring qualities. When affection lessens, as it sooner or later does, we start to see faults and shortcomings and focus on the bad rather than the good. All of a sudden, we do not want to adhere and adjust. We want to be our true self, and we want the other to be what we imagined them to be when we first met them.

When this happens we have to go back to the root of love, which is to see only the good, no matter what the appearance. Change your sense back to the original, wonderful, loving feeling.

I am not saying that we have to love the unpleasant or mean-spirited, but I am saying that you have to see the truth about the other and act accordingly. The truth is that our partners are perfect loving beings no matter what the appearance or behavior.

> **"Love is the foundation from which your decisions about your life should be made."**
> **—Darren L. Johnson**

With this new view of what true love represents, you will experience a shift in the people that are attracted to you. You, in turn, will also be attracted to a different type of personality as you continue to grow.

All mentalities that are on a lesser frequency will move out of your experience as you progress and attract a different set of people.

Naturally, and without any visible doings of yourself, the individuals you will encounter are more loving, kinder, and gentler. They will reflect your newfound loving sense and mirror your recently discovered inner goodness.

"Be unselfish. That is the first and final commandment for those who would be useful and happy in their usefulness. If you think of yourself only, you cannot develop because you are choking the source of development, which is spiritual expansion through thought for others."
—Charles William Eliot

True Love is unselfish and pure

When you truly love, you don't ask for anything in return. You simply love. It becomes your nature. Everything you think, say, and do will be embraced by love.

As you gain a higher sense of Love, you will understand that you must love everyone. You cannot love one and not the other; you cannot pick and choose.

"...because you can!"

Love is Universal; it is good feeling; it is compassion; it is patience; it is caring; it is forgiving; and it is all embracing. It is the mother, or female element, of the Universe and necessary for all creation, giving birth to more good.

Most important, Love is not personal. It is impersonal.

"The happiest people seem to be those who have no particular cause for being happy except that they are so."
—William Ralph Inge

What the world calls love, as earlier pointed out, is mostly only affection or infatuation. There is nothing wrong with affection. Of course you will be affectionate to your loved ones. But Love is a sense of a higher degree, and you will always love relative to your place in unfoldment.

Eventually you will outgrow, so to speak, the affection stage. Love is the ultimate, and it is necessary to reach your life's goal. Universal Love is giving, generous, unselfish, kind, trusting, and all encompassing.

"Beginning today, treat everyone you meet as if they were going to be dead by midnight. Extend to them all the care, kindness and understanding you can muster, and do it with no thought of any reward. Your life will never be the same again."
—Og Mandino

Kindness

Kindness is the gentleness of the Soul. Do an act of kindness, no matter how small, every day, and you will see the results. It will lift your spirits and good feelings will be your reward.

It doesn't take much to be kind and loving. It should be as natural as waking up, walking, or breathing. Because we are wrapped up in the fast-paced, day-to-day race, we often forget that acting kindly is part of our true self.

We forget to stop and ask if we can help someone. It takes only a minute to greet someone, write a thank you card, wave and smile, help someone across the street, or send flowers. It is so easy to brighten someone's day.

Here is a great little story from a man who lives down the street:

Pete's story

"I was at Pavilions buying roses for Ingrid. A young female employee asked who the flowers were for. I said my girlfriend. She told me how lucky that girl was. Nobody had ever bought her flowers. I purchased an extra-long stem red rose, found this woman back by the produce aisle and handed it to her. She was so touched; she followed me out to the parking lot thanking me. What did it cost to bring a smile?"

"...because you can!"

> "Wherever I go, and whoever I encounter, I will bring them a gift. The gift may be a compliment, a flower, or a prayer. Today, I will give something to everyone I come into contact with, and so I will begin the process of circulating joy, wealth and affluence in my life and in the lives of others. Each time I meet someone, I will silently wish them happiness, joy and laughter."
> —*Deepak Chopra*

Practice Love

Love also demands that you forgive and forget. If you for+give, you will for+get—this is a principle of life. If we give, we will get accordingly, so practice giving and practice getting. Accept graciously; everything you get is your reward (good or bad).

You cannot truly love and hold a grudge at the same time. We have to let go of the past and any hurts we've accepted as true. You cannot love with a laden heart.

True Love does not resent or judge others. It knows that the actions of others are only their mistakes. Love knows that you always have to separate the individual from the mistake.

Practice love by looking at your world with loving eyes. Any time a sense or feeling of criticism, hurt, envy, or any unpleasant thought creeps into your mind, say STOP; I will not feel like this again. Going forward I will feel only love. Reverse your inclination, your tendency to think negatively, and your deviation from the truth.

> **"Love is the beauty of the soul."**
> **—*Saint Augustine***

Love yourself first

Self-love is not to be mistaken with Ego.

Self-love means to care about yourself enough physically, emotionally, and spiritually.

Ego cares about material things that can be "shown off," such as status and material riches. Ego identifies itself with worldly status and things. You believe what your Ego tells you.

Self-love is different in that it puts your spiritual health and your unfoldment first, at all times.

Ego puts your personality and who you think you are first. It wants to be better than your neighbor; it wants to have more and more; it is vain.

Self-love is kind and gentle, generous, and at peace.

Ego feeds off external success and vanity, while your self-love seeks confidence and beauty from within.

Love is not selective; in other words, love loves everything and everyone. Love does not discriminate; love is detached, yet love embraces. Love is impersonal. It is Universal.

"...because you can!"

> **"Every time you put your needs last and taking care of self on the back burner; you are denying happiness and self-fulfillment for the most important being in your life: YOU."**
> **—Ilene**

Dependency

Do not make the mistake constantly helping someone out of a crisis for love; it is enabling. Teach others to learn how to take care of themselves. As the old saying goes, "You don't give them fish to eat; you teach them how to fish."

When you love someone, you have his or her best interest in mind, but he or she is still an individual and has to learn how to be self-sufficient. Love is to teach self-sufficiency, how to think better.

Don't bail them out constantly, not even your children. By not allowing them to learn their lessons on their own, you are only hurting them and their unfoldment. You don't give the beggar money; you give him a job.

> **"Truth is a deep kindness that teaches us to be content in our everyday life and share with the people the same happiness."**
> **—Khalil Gibran**

Transform your environment through love

If people would realize that we are of the same substance and quality, then wars, riots, and others types of violence would vanish. We would cherish and respect each other. We would not compete with each other. Instead, we would learn to share, and we would act as one.

If Universal love would be practiced, even only in a small degree by everyone, we would not see the suffering that we see on this plane today. We all would be charitable entities.

We all need to pull together, not just as a nation, but as a Universal Society of Love Consciousness, each of us in our own diverse way, one step at a time. The results will be incredibly beneficial.

It is our responsibility to progress further and further and to gain a better sense of Universal Love. It is our duty to spread the good word. We have to be examples by living this Love. We will, through this pure living, affect the world around us positively.

Build your world, do what you love, find the job you've always wanted, and play and have hobbies. Spend time with your family and friends and, most of all, enjoy…because you can!

"You are an Individuated Aspect of Divinity Itself. The one truth that humanity has found the most difficult to accept is the one truth that would free humanity forever. God and We Are One."
—Neale Donald Walsch

ANSWER THESE QUESTIONS HONESTLY:

1. What does it take to stop hatred in the world?
2. What would happen if we would take care of all of the people around us?
3. Do you think you love enough?
4. Can you see love all around you? Do you look at Nature?
5. What does true love mean to you?
6. Think about the difference between Love and ego. What is ego?
7. What does Universal Love mean to you?
8. How can you show love to others? How can you include all?
9. Is anyone dependant on you? How do you help?
10. Will you take time to practice Love?

CHAPTER 13

WELL-BEING

Health and emotional well-being—what gifts, what treasures!

> "To enjoy good health, to bring true happiness to one's family, to bring peace to all, one must first discipline and control one's own mind. If a man can control his mind he can find the way to Enlightenment, and all wisdom and virtue will naturally come to him."
> —*Buddha*

It stands to reason that if our thinking causes our daily experiences, our thoughts also cause our health and sickness.

I am not a doctor, scientist, or healthcare professional. I have however, over the years, proven to myself that my health is directly related to my thoughts. My mental moods, emotions, thought habits, and, most of all, the beliefs I carry about my health are the cause of my well-being, or, conversely, woe in exact proportion to those mental attitudes.

"...because you can!"

Doctors and scientists agree that stress causes most of our illnesses. We seem to live in stress-filled times. Daily life is packed with competition, anxiety, hectic schedules, and exhaustion. Even the attempt to live simply seems at times stressful.

Fear also plays a huge factor in all health-related issues. Fear must be eradicated completely before healing can take place. Fear intensifies pain; fear makes you weak and vulnerable. Fear freezes your otherwise reasonable thought.

It is a giant and a daunting task to reason out your fears created by monster illnesses like cancer, but it can be done. Shedding your fears is the first step to healing. It makes you think clearer about what needs to be done. It gives you courage.

We will take on this task throughout our journey step by step. To give you an example how widespread fear reaches, even in lesser, more common physical ailments such as a cold, we are afraid of the discomfort. Or maybe we're afraid of losing time at work or passing the cold on to our children or co-workers, which, in turn, causes more stress.

We are not really aware that we are afraid, but we are. It is a vicious cycle.

"It is health that is real wealth and not pieces of gold and silver."
—Mohandas Gandhi

Hurry, worry, and stress

Hurry, worry, and stress are twenty-first-century diseases, and the medical field strongly agrees that most all illnesses are stress related. The whole world seems to run on hurry, worry, and fear. You hurry to work; you hurry to get your errands done. You worry about your children, your job performance, and your spouse's illness. You stress over the bills.

Hurry, distractions, and worry cause accidents such as falling, tripping, car crashes, and so on.

Stress, for example, is known to cause backaches, tenseness, headaches and migraines, premature aging and gray hair, high blood pressure, and so forth. Stress can also cause skin irritations, eczema, and hives. These are just a few examples.

Do you remember any stressful time in your life that expressed itself as a physical illness? What does stress do to you physically? Do you see the connection between your stressful thinking and your physical well-being?

For years I wanted a promotion at my previous job, but it was a slow, corporate process and the stress of feeling "left behind" and "not appreciated" caused my head to explode, literally. I developed migraines that were at times unbearable. I was so uptight about it that my back muscles were in a constant spasm. It went on for a long period but I did not correlate the two; I thought I was just a migraine sufferer like so many others.

But once I received my promotion and all was settled, the migraines disappeared over night and I never had one again. Now that I know the cause, I will never experience another migraine.

Other stressful times followed this incident. However, as I learned to handle each situation with a more calm and confident attitude, I did not manifest the corresponding unhealthy conditions.

"Thinking of disease constantly will intensify it. Feel always I'm healthy in body and mind."
—Swami Sivananda

Skin

Skin irritations are your reaction to other people and situations: close friends or family members, your environment, your daily work, and every day occurrences. It's on the surface; you are literally letting things get under your skin. You feel distress or harassment. We all know that shingles come from stress. The same is true with hives and other rashes, so it makes sense that all skin issues are related to similar kinds of dispositions and uneasy thoughts.

Another personal experience I had many years ago was a stress-related issue that manifested in a skin rash all over my face, right out in the open for everyone to see. At the time, a new boss was hired, and she was a rather unpleasant lady.

She came into a well-established department and was demeaning and demanding, to say the least. Instead of seeing who she really was, I reacted emotionally and took everything personally. As a result, my skin broke out. It was the external reflection of tension and hurt feelings boiling within.

As I said, skin issues are related to "letting things get under your skin," and reacting to outside issues. Being irritated, itching to do something, impatience, and in some cases anger, all play a part in it.

Having it show up in a visible place, such as the face, indicates that you want everyone to know how you feel.

If it's on your back or on a body part that's covered by clothing, you probably want to hide your distress from others or yourself. Either way, it can be cured by self-praise, self-love, a more sensible attitude and, most of all, by not taking everything so personally.

You have to deal with life's situations in a calm and comforting way.

How do you react to criticism? Does it bother you what others think of you or say about you? Let it go; it's not important. Go on with your business, and let them stew in their own discordant sense of self. You need to stop reacting to others and their opinions.

> "...because you can!"

> "It makes no sense to worry about things you have no control over because there's nothing you can do about them, and why worry about things you do control? The activity of worrying keeps you immobilized."
> **—Wayne Dyer**

Stomach

Humankind's hot temper and anger cause many stomach issues such as ulcers and stomach bleeding. Stomach disorders are a widespread medical condition, usually relating to being upset at someone or something. It also relates to an exaggerated sense of unreasonableness.

Haven't we all experienced an uptight stomach after a fight with a friend or a nervous stomach before an interview or a public speech? Many times we experience diarrhea when we are nervous or experiencing a sense of exaggerated emotion. The truth is, we are taking the circumstances too personally and are being too emotional about it.

Unreasonableness and stubbornness, on the opposite side of the spectrum, are also related to upset stomachs. They cause intestinal problems, which can lead to hemorrhoids and bowel issues.

We now know that fear intensifies pain. Your fear causes you to panic and imagine it to be real. The more fear you have about an illness, the more real and incurable it seems to you.

All of it, as you can see, is caused in your mind.

"Holding on to anger is like grasping a hot coal with the intent of throwing it at someone else; you are the one who gets burned."
—Buddha

Accidents

Accidents and falls are usually caused by haphazard thinking, not paying attention, absentmindedness, and a break in harmony in your mentality (i.e., fights, arguments, and the like).

No one is naturally accident-prone, as people call it. Your uneasy, unstable, and distracted thoughts are what cause accidents. And when something like this happens to you, brush yourself off to the best of your ability and move on. Don't dwell on what just happened. It is your belief of swelling and bruising and all the expected discomfort that will cause your demise.

One sunny day in LA, I went on my morning jog, just a brisk twenty-minute walk through the lovely neighborhood. I was feeling good, admiring the perfectly manicured lawns and gardens.

As I got closer to my destination, an older gentleman came out of his driveway. From the corner of my eye, I saw that he reminded me of an old, unpleasant client from a past job.

During that one moment of negative, critical thought, which took me away from the pleasures of the morning air and the enjoyment of the freshness and vigor I felt, I stumbled and fell. I hit the pavement hard, in slow-motion. The stranger asked me politely if I was okay. He was concerned and caring, nothing like I remembered the old client to be; he only looked like him.

Embarrassed, I got up and knew that really nothing had happened to me. I had just made a mistake. This was a picture of immediate effect caused by my wrong, critical thought—instant punishment you might say. As I took responsibility for my actions, I pulled myself together quickly.

I didn't look at my wounds and just kept walking home (you might call it hopping), determined to know I was alright. I did what I had planned to do during the day, ignoring the original swelling and bruising and pain, never fearing any harm and never talking to anyone, including my husband, about what happened.

I wanted the visible signs to be gone by the time he came home from work. I wanted to prove to myself again, as I have done so many times, that I can heal myself. I understand that healing yourself even of the visible signs of injury takes practice and understanding, but it is possible.

You can do this also; you have what it takes!

By the end of the day, all swelling and bruising and pain were gone, but a small scar on my knee served as a reminder of my "exercise of the day." As I am writing this a few hours later, I am perfectly fine.

"Health is the greatest possession. Contentment is the greatest treasure. Confidence is the greatest friend. Non-being is the greatest joy."
—Lao Tzu

Cuts

You can do a similar treatment if you cut yourself (and I'm not talking about cutting off your limbs).

As soon as you injure yourself, say "stop!" and mean it. Do not fear. Again, you have to be fearless. Know "nothing really happened" as you are a mental being and not a solid body. Don't look at it. Looking at wounds make them more real to you, and what you see will leave a mental impression.

Know that you are alright, and then forget about it. Be not afraid, as fear is a magnifier. Do not dwell on it, don't talk about it, and don't show it to everyone around you.

Nature will take care of it and heal you perfectly in time. Remember not to show your "war wounds." Please do these exercises only if you are convinced that this will work for you. Go to a doctor if you feel the need to have it looked at or think that you need medical attention. Remember we are only in Kindergarten, and you don't have to prove anything to anyone but yourself.

As the memory fades away, so does the scar. If you continue to tell the story, the scar will stay to prove your condition. It is lodged in your mind. Let it go, you don't need to be reminded of hurts. Your memory should contain only the lovely, the good, and the perfect moments in your life.

"A scar is nothing more than a memory of a hurt."
—*William W. Walter*

Alcoholism

Another widespread disease is alcoholism, and as psychiatrists have established, the disease stems from a lack of self-love and a lack of maturity, and it is a form of escape. People's emotional development stops when their habitual drinking or drug abuse starts.

Indeed, it is a mental disease that must be treated by a professional therapist, but it cannot be healed unless a patient is able to change his or her mentality. We are accustomed to treat the symptoms with only medications, and that is why many addictions are so hard to cure.

"Without health life is not life; it is only a state of languor and suffering—an image of death."
—*Buddha*

Depression

Depression equals not loving life. Depressed individuals do not have enough interest in life, experience constant negative feelings, and feel hopeless. It is vital that they find love and interest in life in order to be healed.

Appreciation of even the smallest things in life will help to lift them to a better frame of mind. Turning negativity in tiny portions into positive specks of light and hope is a starting point.

> **"It is health that is real wealth and not pieces of gold and silver."**
> **—Mohandas Gandhi**

Obesity

Food is a wonderful treat and here to enjoy. There are limitless dishes, flavors, and recipes for your pleasure. You should experiment, try new foods, and discover exotic tastes, but when food is being used as a pacifier or stress reliever, you are misunderstanding its purpose.

When you overeat and consume large quantities without pleasure and fill yourself with junk and unnecessary weight, it becomes an addictive obsession. No amount of food will satisfy your starving mind.

You are trying to feel better because you are lacking self-worth and self- love. You constantly have the need to fulfill, or fill full, your lacking self-esteem. You have a donut hole inside of you, as a psychiatrist of a friend of mine once put it.

"...because you can!"

You will never be fully satisfied until you have found your inner mental food. Your nourishment has to come from the soul.

Of course, this extreme illness can also be a cry for more attention, reflecting more serious issues. It is an imbalance in mind, obsessive craving, extreme longing for love, and a sense of going overboard.

Like all other mental dependency cases, therapy is strongly suggested to get to the underlying core issues.

> **"Health is the greatest gift, contentment the greatest wealth, faithfulness the best relationship."**
> **—Buddha**

Addictions of any kind

Much has been written about the opulence of this society and the excess that it has brought to our daily living. Excess or addictions of any kind stem from an unsatisfied and immature mind. It also represents a longing to escape from responsibilities. Individuals with these afflictions stopped their emotional development at the time of addiction. They stayed as little boys or girls and are not able to cope with normal daily responsibilities.

A "fulfilling of the soul" rather than reaching out to material remedies is needed.

If you are prone to any of the above examples, you should start looking for things that make you feel good. The accomplishment of a certain goal you wanted to achieve might be a good start to help you reach that good feeling.

What makes you feel good might be different from what makes someone else feel good. Maybe you enjoy working out at the gym, walking in the park, playing music, reading, or maybe you enjoy just doing nothing and relaxing. Maybe you wanted to remodel your house or find a new, more fulfilling job. Being able to do this will make you feel fulfilled and happy. It will empower you.

There is no such thing as "I don't feel well" to the Universal substance, which you are part of. Do you think the Universe ever feels shitty?

And ask yourself this: "Do I like 'it' [whatever the illness is] enough to keep it?" Ask this question in anything you do. It will open your eyes, literally.

I have given you some reasonable examples of illnesses caused by mental means alone, thus looking deeper would reveal a wealth of connections between thought and disease, invisible cause and visible effect. This is a starting point, however, and much more needs to be solved.

"A wise man should consider that health is the greatest of human blessings, and learn how by his own thought to derive benefit from his illnesses."
—*Hippocrates*

Negative dispositions and feelings

Left unattended, all negative feelings can and will lead to illness. They include jealousy, hate, envy, hopelessness, resentment, and stubbornness—you name it! This list goes on and on.

Negativity must be turned into positivity. Your wrong perceptions have to be reasoned out, and your sense has to be lifted to a better frame of mind. All dispositions can be reasoned out by allowing your mind to let in the light of Truth.

Negative and wrong feelings are the most powerful as they are the multipliers. You have to stop them as soon as you feel them surfacing. "No, I will not feel like this ever again!" Be strong, be forceful, be truthful, and be courageous. Defeat this negative ripple effect.

> **"The first wealth is health."**
> **—*Ralph Waldo Emerson***

Guilt

Guilt, another strong ill feeling and cause of illness, is thought of by most people as the voice of good conscience. You know what is right or wrong, so take charge of your own affairs. You instinctively know what you have to do when guilt sets in.

Do not let others run your life or make you feel guilty; they don't know what's best for you. Make decisions for yourself, and govern your own affairs wisely. When you live your life within these rules, guilt will not be a part of your daily feelings.

There is nothing to be guilty about in the first place. Any mistake you make is just that: a mistake. Correct the error and then move on. Give no more thought to the slip-up. Each moment is a brand new chance to start a new beginning. Take that chance and run with it!

You will never have to feel guilty if you live righteously by your own conscience!

"If you look into your own heart, and you find nothing wrong there, what is there to worry about? What is there to fear?"
—*Confucius*

Self-condemnation

Self-condemnation is another mental poison that robs you of your vitality and energy. You might think of yourself as less than because maybe you acted immaturely and did something that hurt someone, or you were brought up to believe that you were not smart enough. There are too many wrong childhood imposed impressions and taught feelings that you need to clear out of your mind. You have to reprogram yourself, starting right now.

You are a spiritual, perfect mental being. Love yourself, be proud of yourself, and surely your world will improve as your sense of self improves.

"...because you can!"

"A life lived of choice is a life of conscious action. A life lived of chance is a life of unconscious creation."
—Neale Donald Walsch

The power of a name

We have a name for everything, including all sicknesses. Just watch the advertisements and their never-ending remedies, cures, and pills for any ailment. Many we haven't even heard of before. It is one of the biggest businesses in the United States, and certainly all over the world.

We have a name for every symptom, hoping that by knowing "what" it is, we can find a cure. However, this is making it into something and giving it means, rather than just knowing that it is only the visible manifestation of uneasy thinking.

We call the accompanying pain, for example, a migraine or headache, heartburn, sore muscles, and so on. The name you give your ailments will make the unwanted negative image seemingly more real and further intensify the pain of the already ailing body.

Naming a symptom evokes an image and makes it more tangible to you. It gives it substance. Mention the name of any disease, such as AIDS, and immediately you have a dreadful image of symptoms, suffering, and pain. Talk about measles or eczema, and you will see skin irritations. Imagine cancer and you think radiation, loss of hair, and so forth.

On the other side of the spectrum, mention a name of a beautiful place and you will see loveliness and maybe a feeling of calm and peace will accompany this picture. So you see this is imagination at its best and worst. The name will create a vivid picture in your mind, no matter if it's a positive or negative image.

Many people are not even aware of their power to make themselves sick, or to heal themselves. The idea that you can make yourself sick will probably make some of you cringe. It will fill you with fear, or you will immediately deny it. But it is a fact.

"As a cure for worrying, work is better than whiskey."
—Ralph Waldo Emerson

The sheer belief in sickness

As a reminder, we must empty out the outgrown beliefs about sickness and health and let go of the belief that we are victims. Instead we are victors, here to rediscover our true inheritance. We inherit a healthy, wealthy, and happy life on this plane of existence. We have to remember and reestablish this concept firmly in our minds.

The sheer belief in sickness will make you vulnerable to disease. Be strong and support your natural healthy being by learning the truth. Start understanding the Laws instead of buying into beliefs. Start living right by controlling diet, exercising, reducing stress, yoga, meditation, stillness time, and any other activity that makes *you* feel good and whole.

"...because you can!"

"Health is not a condition of matter, but of Mind."
—*Mary Baker Eddy*

How do you treat the lesser ailments in life?

Peaceful, loving, and calm thinking is the answer as well as not allowing outside influences get to you in the first place. What's important is not listening to the opinions of others, but rather knowing that all things will be dealt with in due time and that Universal goodness is always with you.

Practice a balanced, kind, and loving personality when dealing with everyone. Don't be selective in who you treat kindly.

Stop judging and condemning! Wish everyone well and send them good thoughts. Be on your way cheerfully, working on your own unfoldment.

Carve out a piece of heaven in your lifetime, here and now. Don't chime in with the negative forces around you. Don't watch too much of the news as it's always unpleasant drama. Don't search out violent movies or play slayer video games, as all of those choices affect your subconscious.

Your subconscious will store and act out your feelings and emotions you took in by watching and observing those negative impressions. You might say that you are not subjective to those impressions, but your subconscious registers everything and will play it back when the time comes. Cherish yourself and your body. Live healthy!

> **"To keep the body in good health is a duty... otherwise we shall not be able to keep our mind strong and clear."**
> **—Buddha**

You are living your life under the rules of the Laws of Life

Cause and Effect, Thought and Manifestation. You are punished for every mistake and rewarded for every good thought, be it small or large.

This is not to scare you, only to show you the importance of correcting your thoughts and feelings. It is only your lack of understanding of the Law and its workings that prevents you from recognizing that all the headaches, backaches, stomach trouble, diseased conditions, financial setbacks, and relationship problems that you experience are the direct result of your occasional or habitual violations of the Laws of Nature.

Repeat right now and every day, "I am perfect right now," "Good is with me always," "I am improving and multiplying my inherent goodness," and "I am well."

During this daily practice, heal your sense of the "other." There is no "other" as we are all one. Think of yourself as a Universal being. Not separate, "a-lone" but "all-one." You are an individual, yet part of the whole. Keep your awareness wide awake. And most of all, rest for wellness and "let your soul catch up," as a friend of mine put it.

You heal not only your sense of sickness, but also your relationships, finances, family discord, your short comings, and your sense of all that is not perfect and good. Think better about any situation, and let go of the picture that you hold in mind.

God, the "I AM," is the healer and creator. Free yourself from unpleasant creations. You made it; therefore, you can undo it!

> "No one saves us but ourselves. No one can and no one may. We ourselves must walk the path."
> —*Buddha*

Spiritual consciousness or right consciousness is the creator of all

Consciousness is the creator of all. You are consciousness, part of Universal consciousness and, therefore, also the creator of your health and well-being.

Even in cases of faith healing, thought (conscious activity) is the creator. Your strong faith and your belief in the power of being healed through an outside power is what heals you. However, if you don't comprehend the Laws of Life, the ailment will recur since you have not healed your understanding. Faith healing is not permanent; understanding healing is.

> **"The wish for healing has always been half of health."**
> *—Lucius Annaeus Seneca*

Real or true faith is not blind faith. True Faith is Understanding or the faith in Truth. It is faith that all will work out no matter what the situation, knowing the truth of Universal perfection.

Real faith is a sense of confidence in the all power of your thought. We have to identify ourselves with having the ability and potential already within. The "kingdom" is within, not without.

Faith is an attitude; it is a certain way of thinking. Faith is the knowing that everything you desire already exists as a possibility in mind. It is a certainty of things yet to come.

> **"To believe in a just law of cause and effect, carrying with it a punishment or a reward, is to believe in righteousness."**
> *—Ernest Holmes*

Don't think about your body and its appearance- look only at your mental dispositions

To correct the visible error on the body, the disturbed mentality has to be corrected. All sickness and suffering is self-induced or self-imposed and, therefore, you can self-correct. This is not something you learn in a day or two. It is a lifetime commitment to the truth. This statement is not meant to be harsh or judgmental; it is purely a statement of truth.

"...because you can!"

The mind leaves its visible imprint on the body, so we must cease thinking imperfect thoughts and correct our habits and mental moods. We must always have in front of us a perfect image of our self and of what we want to experience. We have to know and accept the complete control that mind has over the body, as many Metaphysicians have pointed out in the past.

All so-called chronic ailments and diseases are caused by long standing, habitual thoughts like grudges, resentments, hate, fear, worry, and similar dispositions. Feelings gone wrong also express themselves as illness and discomfort.

As pointed out earlier, accidents are no accidents. They are caused mostly by haphazard, careless, or absentminded thoughts and behavior.

Constantly dwell on the good side of life. Pay no attention to appearance and hold steadfast in your heart the world you would like to see and experience.

"You and I are essentially infinite choice-makers. In every moment of our existence, we are in that field of all possibilities where we have access to an infinity of choices."
—*Deepak Chopra*

Harmony will affect your well-being; it is a state of wellness

Harmony is Heaven; therefore, think harmonious thoughts. The kingdom of heaven is within you and no place else—not outside of you but within you. You only have to look.

We also make our own hell through ignorance. Hell is not real; it is only a lack of good or a lesser sense of good, all changeable by you. Hell is a discordant or inharmonious mental state.

You can overcome any circumstance be it poverty, illness, or unhappiness. Throw away your old beliefs and start now, step by step, one day at a time. Make each thought better than the thought before, and chip away at it. Your life experience will improve, and the end result will be marvelous.

Create your heaven on earth NOW; do not put it off for later. Now is the time and always will be. Enjoy now and every step of the way. You are here to grow and unfold from within yourself. Life is progression; it is not static, and it does not go backward—only forward. Life is a series of events, and you'll want to express more and more of your inherent good throughout this process.

Well-being is a harmonious mental state: a state of bliss, good feelings, loving feelings, clean living, and the development of a well-balanced character. Good is a mental quality, a sense of harmony. It is only our lack of understanding that sends us to the doctor, to the divorce court, or the bankruptcy court.

Repeat this to yourself every day: "I know that I am the total source of all that befalls me every day of my life, including my health and well-being. Nothing and no one can cause for me. The change in my thinking and the tuning into the Universal source will heal me of discord, be it in health, wealth, or happiness."

"I find hope in the darkest of days, and focus in the brightest. I do not judge the universe."
—Dalai Lama

Your healthful and youthful attitude going forward

Mind works as a trinity: Mind or Consciousness, Thought as its activity, and Understanding which produces the effects of your thought convictions.

Health includes vitality, youthfulness, playfulness, clean living, and a loving heart. A youthful attitude, curiosity, and enthusiasm for Life is what you need to stay young and healthy.

Our minds stay young; it is our sense of time that ages us. We believe that it is natural for us to grow old and die. But this is another mistaken concept. It is a human belief.

"You can free yourself from aging by reinterpreting your body and by grasping the link between belief and biology."
—Deepak Chopra

Our problem is that we let the mind slow down, that we think we have to retire and spend more time on the couch watching television. Many beliefs, including not being able to eat certain foods or that it is natural to acquire certain old age illnesses, start to kick in.

We see years of experience as aging, instead of as maturing. Maturity is natural and good. With maturity you hopefully gain Wisdom and, as Socrates said a long time ago, "Wisdom is the principle thing."

The mind does not grow old; it's your sense of time passing that produces this illusion.

Your sense of youth comes from the love of life, being inquisitive, a love of learning, and your looking forward to a new day. We mentally start believing that the vitality of youth is no longer with us, but I'm sure that if you ask a group of fifty to sixty-year-olds, they'd tell you that they wouldn't want to be twenty again.

Maturity brings with it a sense of stability, security, spiritual calmness, and contentment.

Don't fall into the trap of believing and sensing old age, getting into a rut, or thinking you know it all because you've been through it all.

With this rigid attitude we become inflexible, and stiffness shows up in your mentality as well as in your body. Keep your thinking fresh with enthusiasm, let it flow easily and freely, and have a zest for life.

Your world is your consciousness objectified, including your mental picture of aging.

"...because you can!"

I think these examples make clear that most physical ailments are the result of negative or sick thinking, so change your thought perceptions today...because you can!

**"The universal Mind contains all knowledge.
It is the potential ultimate of all things.
To it, all things are possible."
—*Ernest Holmes***

ANSWER THESE QUESTIONS HONESTLY:

1. How is your well-being at this time? What do you need to improve?
2. Do you see the connection between your stressful thinking and your physical condition?
3. How do you react to criticism?
4. What do you think is the cause of addictions and how should they be treated?
5. What are some strong, positive affirmations for well-being?
6. What are you feeling guilty about? How can you change it?
7. Who is the creator and who is the healer?
8. What is your sense of aging? How can you achieve a youthful sense?
9. What does maturity mean to you? What are the qualities that come with maturity?
10. Staying flexible and full of vigor will produce what? How much interest in life do you have?

CHAPTER 14

THE UNIVERSE

"There is an orderliness in the universe, there is an unalterable law governing everything and every being that exists or lives. It is no blind law; for no blind law can govern the conduct of living beings."
—*Mohandas Gandhi*

What happened?

The invisible Universe or Mass Consciousness has always existed. Based on the best available measurements as of 2011, the original visible state of the Universe existed around 13.7 billion years ago, which is often referred to as the time when the Big Bang occurred.

We also think that civilization as we know it today started around 3,000 years ago. Historians write, "Our knowledge of prehistory derives from surviving objects—the evidence of archaeology. History, by contrast, is based on documents. These various interconnections

"...because you can!"

mean that history, civilization and writing all begin at the same time. That time is about 3,100 BC."

This brief timeframe of "the starting point" of civilization, compared to the timeline of the existence of the Universe, is a very short period of time and creates a stunning perspective.

At first glance, humankind might seem like an insignificant speck in the solar system. However, the Universe tells us we have value and roles to play and contributions to make to the harmony of Oneness. We can see that in the power of our own thoughts.

So all things considered, compared to the existence of modern civilization, don't you think we have barely begun to explore life in general, ourselves, and have only begun to understand ourselves?

Have we not merely scratched the surface of life's meaning, of our own calling and purpose? Not to mention understanding the Universe and its Laws? We are babies in the grand scheme, barely born. We humans are but infants and still gawking at the world around us.

New Thought, or focusing and containing the belief of powerful thinking, was not openly discussed until the mid 1800s. Many new "Laws of Mind" discoveries have been made since then.

> **"The Universe is worked and guided from within outwards."**
> *—H. P. Blavatsky*

Observe and ask yourself, "What does the Universe consist of?"

The Universe, or what we see, is merely a shadow of mass consciousness objectified. It is alive; it is energy. It always has been and always will be. It is a vast ocean of infinite consciousness with infinite power.

It always works perfectly and naturally.

Its innate urge is to constantly cause and unfold more of itself; it is Life expressed. It is one gigantic living being, and it constantly multiplies more of itself.

**"The universe must exist for the self-expression of God and the delight of God."
—Ernest Holmes**

What is our relationship to the Universe?

More and more people are awakening to the fact that there is a non-personal Universal power behind all of creation. It is flowing through us, a part of us, and directing us to the point of perfect Understanding of who and what we are. When once fully understood, the results will be marvelous.

Our relationship is intimate and an integral part of this innate urge for Universal expression. We are a living part of this living organism.

Look at these simple examples: the abundance of seeds in plant life, the countless species of the animal kingdom, and the births of our children. Look at this grand picture of our Universe and its limitless possibilities!

Yes, it is *our* Universe. We are part of it, and we are co-creators. In infinite consciousness, there is also infinite power for you to access and use to your liking. You might not ever need it or use it, but it's there for the taking. This creative power is yours, whenever you want it.

> **"But in reality we are accompanied by the whole dancing universe."**
> **—*Ruth St. Denis***

Of course you need to know how to use this force for the good. You can use it for other than good purposes, but it will surely backfire. The consequences may be negative and unexpected.

The "how" is the key to manifestation of your desired goods. You can repeat all the positive affirmations all day long, but if you cannot apply the thoughts properly, then nothing in your life will change. Application, application, application—this is your tool!

I will ask you many questions throughout this book. Consider them seriously. They are tools that encourage you to delve deeper into your consciousness to find the answers.

The Law of Cause and Effect, or Like attracts Like, will ensure that you receive what you imagine to be true. It is impartial and will act upon your thoughts and convictions, good or bad. It does not differentiate. It does not know the difference; it only responds.

Our developing minds do not yet grasp the vastness and, many times, stand in the way of natural unfoldment. Let it happen. Work with it, not against it!

Use your knowledge, no matter how little

Even though your understanding is relative at this time, use what you do know for the time being. Use it for your good: embrace it, flow with it, and learn from it.

Let yourself feel the creative flow that is constantly pushing for expression through you. Be a wave in this ocean of life's ceaseless motion, and move naturally with it. Offer no resistance. Be still.

> **"We can hear the silent voice of the spiritual universe within our own hearts."**
> —*Ruth St. Denis*

In this beginning state, honesty—with yourself and others—is most important. In your search for the truth and self-improvement, you will have to face the facts. In order to change your world you have to start within yourself and be totally open and forthcoming. You have to unlock all the hidden resentments, grudges, past pains, and sufferings and clear them out, one by one.

You don't have to tell anyone about it. Better yet, DO NOT tell anyone about it as the opinions of others, even loved ones, will slow you down.

Enjoy the method of creation. It is part of your development and growth. If you analyze your project or desire, one step at a time, you will learn by experience, and your conclusions and thought convictions will be more real to you. Hence, your outcome or manifestations accompanied by an intense feeling of love for your good desire will harden into fact quicker.

> **"Because our entire universe is made up of consciousness, we never really experience the universe directly, we just experience our consciousness of the universe, our perception of it, so right, our only universe is perception."**
> *—Alan Moore*

Remember, you can change your path at any time!

If during your journey a new direction appears and this path feels right to pursue, follow your instincts.

Ask yourself if it is good for all concerned. Is it beautiful, lovely, or helpful? Does it feel right? If the answer is yes, then go for it. You are making right choices. Move on it.

Your life's journey is one choice at a time.

> **"May you live your life as if the maxim of your actions were to become universal law."**
> *—Immanuel Kant*

Can we know all?

None of the spiritual writers—present or past—are the ultimate knowers. Each author or poet has developed a good understanding relative to his or her unfoldment at the time of writing.

They might be ahead of many of us in this journey. And they might have had more knowledge than most, I grant you. Still, what they know is relative and not the ultimate Understanding.

However, they (and we) cannot know all there is to know for the following reasons: life is progressive and limitless, and Unfoldment will go on forever.

There are serial dimensions, or states of consciousness, that we have yet to explore after we have mastered this state of earthly life. "There are many mansions in my father's house," as Jesus pointed out. We are only at the beginning state or dimension. This is only the schoolmaster state, Kindergarten you might say.

"Life on earth is a Kindergarten for Image making."
—*Neville*

Life, since it is of the universal substance, is made out of ultimate Intelligence. Since you are part of this life force, you are intelligent by nature. Do you acknowledge this fact?

You might not comprehend all of Intelligence at this point, but you are expressing this power to some degree. You are using this intelligence to become more intelligent, and you are expressing it in the exact proportion of your Understanding of it.

Through this Understanding, even though it may be only a partial or limited Understanding, you can improve your environment and relationships to others.

The desire of Life is to give more Life. The desire of Love is to give more Love. As your sense of Life and Love improve, so will your life experience in exact proportion.

> **"The universal Mind contains all knowledge.
> It is the potential ultimate of all things.
> To it, all things are possible."
> —Ernest Holmes**

Thought vibrations

Many of you might have read *The Secret* by Rhonda Byrne and, as she correctly points out, your thoughts are frequencies, permeating through the Universe. The better, more refined thoughts you think are higher thought vibrations and will negate lower thought vibrations, which are the lesser or wrong thoughts you think.

The higher frequency of being, or being "up" in the scale of being, is the desired state. Higher frequency thoughts include loving and kind thoughts, happy and grateful thoughts, abundant and generous thoughts, as well as a healthy attitude.

There is infinite Intelligence and boundless Wisdom within us. All we have to do is to access and contact it by thinking those higher thoughts.

Let it in. It will inspire you, lift you up, guide you, and heal you. It will show you the way if you'd only listen carefully and act on your instincts.

By applying these higher frequencies, you can alter your future positively. The future is flexible and can be altered through your concept of self. It can be changed through your letting go of lower frequency thoughts and feelings. Don't forget to keep these feelings in check!

Any changes are taking place in consciousness first and have to be solidified in your mind to the point of conviction.

At every moment of our lives, we have a choice. Depending on the choice made, our future will correspond. Therefore, it is imperative that we shape our future in our mind and conform to the harmony in our desire.

"Life is a mirror and will reflect back to the thinker what he thinks into it."
—*Ernest Holmes*

The world that we think is so solidly real

What we call earth and the planets are but a shadow of mass consciousness. It is mental in origin and nature.

"...because you can!"

Our own beliefs that the earth and the planets are solid and certain convictions about the world that are not in agreement with the truth become our experience.

This conviction, that all is solid and composed of matter, expresses itself in our daily life. However, it does not make it a fact.

As pointed out on numerous occasions, our world is changeable at any time through our own thought modifications, and mass consciousness can change a larger world picture.

"The creation of a thousand forests is in one acorn."
—*Ralph Waldo Emerson*

Identify yourself with your ideal

First you must know what your ideal is. Give it lots of careful thought and it will come to you. It might be a simple life. It might be a loving relationship that you crave most, or it might be a glamorous life in the spotlight. It is all achievable as this world, which you think is so solidly real, is only a mirror of your imagination.

Start in small steps and as you prove it to yourself, your self-confidence will grow in proportion to your sense acquired. Live and act on this conviction, always looking forward. Do not waver, doubt, or question. Go back to your source and know that all good desire must come to pass; it is the Law of the Universe.

All new concepts of yourself will also result in a changed relationship with your world. Your whole picture will change accordingly, including your relationships with people and your daily environment. Remember, the people that you experience and your environment are also mental; they are a reflection of you.

So as soon as we succeed in transforming ourselves, the world will magically change into a harmonious state, conforming to our new perspective. We can absolutely rely on this Law to give us exactly that which is our nature. "As within, so without," everything starts within first before it is manifested without. Remember this!

If during this process you experience pain, a set back of any kind, or some other unpleasantness, look over your own shoulder (or maybe in the mirror) and do not blame anyone or anything else for your shortcomings. You are the only cause in your life's experience.

Pick yourself up and brush yourself off, and then continue the journey to happiness. You are already on the right path!

**"Even sleepers are workers and collaborators in what goes on in the Universe."
—*Heraclitus***

God, Intelligence, You, has have no needs

The Mind, Consciousness—or, you might call it God—is an intelligent power that has no needs. It is

"...because you can!"

perfect and complete. However, its purpose is to express itself through you, thereby fulfilling your desires.

Your correct thought, being the activity of your individual consciousness, will fulfill your ideals when applied correctly. Use this concept of Universal power to your advantage.

Hold the position in mind that you are a complete particle of the Universal substance. You are the whole. Within you is all the power necessary for your betterment. What a feeling of freedom! What a feeling of strength and courage!

On a personal level, never put yourself in the position of need. Never see yourself as lacking anything. No matter what the appearance, always see yourself creating and fulfilling your desires. You are a wishing-well.

Comprehension does not know the difference. It will give you what you want, be it good or bad.

> **"The man form is higher than the angel form; of all forms it is the highest. Man is the highest being in creation, because he aspires to freedom."**
> **—*Paramahansa Yogananda***

Don't wait until you are sixty, seventy, or eighty to ask about the meaning of life

Ask now, no matter your age. Agreed, it takes a somewhat mature mind to grasp the importance of

Universal love, mind over matter, and other modern thought, concepts, and ideas.

I have found that there are many people who are more open to new concepts these days, and I can see a huge change in Universal consciousness. Just look at the Internet, at social media, and in book stores at what's available to you today.

A great shift in awareness is going on right now. What an exciting time!

Universal consciousness is cause, as well as mental substance, of the entire objectified world. Your consciousness, with its thought activity, is the cause of your specific world. You are a world within yourself.

As I am writing this, I am certain that this life experience I am sensing at this moment is "my world" that I have created for myself. It is my sense of myself, my sense of my home, my sense of my environment. It is my sense of my life.

"And we're seeing a higher level of consciousness and many more opportunities for people to challenge their present ways of thinking and move into a grander and larger experience of who they really are."
—Neale Donald Walsch

Your body and your soul

The visible form of your organized, systematized self is your body. In other words, your body is your visible, yet mental shadow of your thought convictions. We have to stop believing the mistaken idea that our bodies are solid. We have to let go of the misconception that our minds and our bodies are two separate things. They are one and the same—one as cause and one as effect.

Neither the body nor the brain can think. It is the Soul, your Consciousness that does the thinking and the creating, manifesting, and healing.

You are a mental being!

**"All the principles of heaven and earth are living inside you. Life itself is truth, and this will never change. Everything in heaven and earth breathes. Breath is the thread that ties creation together."
—Morihei Ueshiba**

Synchronicity in the Universe

Synchronicity plays a big part in this game of life. When you are tuned in to the flow of the Universe, you will experience Synchronicity. You might think of a friend and the phone rings; you might think of a certain subject and the answer comes in the mail; you might have a question, and the news anchor just happens to talk about it.

For everything you do or want, the time has to be right. The Universe knows; it takes patience and it takes courage to allow things to happen rather than

The Universe

to force them. You might be on pins and needles about a specific desire, and it just doesn't seem to work out. You are anxious and impatient, and then all of a sudden, one day, it happens. The pieces fall into place, and everything works out perfectly.

It would have worked out perfectly without your stress and anxiety. So what was the purpose of your stressing over the situation?

"Stress is nothing more than a socially acceptable form of mental illness."
—Richard Carlson

We have to understand how the mind works in order to enjoy the fruits forever!

My intent is to provide you with the tools to shape your destiny and to clarify the necessary steps. Open your spiritual eyes, listen to your inner ear, and open your mind. No matter how many doubts and fears enter your mind, brush them aside. Sit quietly at peace and allow your inner self to show you the right way.

Universal life is forever, and the fulfilling of the Law is your destiny!

"Teach and practice, practice and teach— that is all we have; that is all we are good for; that is all we ever ought to do."
—Ernest Holmes

"...because you can!"

The memory of the past is just a dream

"It," whatever "it" was, has passed. But you are in the NOW, and now is all there is.

Your memory is your sense of what has happened. It is the accumulation of sensory experiences, one moment at a time.

Everyone has a different sense and remembers events slightly differently. This memory or sense changes over time. It is not necessary to hang on to it, or bury it, or re-live it. It is the past. It will not and cannot come back.

If you created a good memory, cherish it but move on and live in the now. Right here and now you can create more good memories. Use your past experiences to build better experiences.

Our subconscious stores everything, knowingly or not. All impressions received, all words spoken, and all feelings felt are faithfully recorded and tucked away into this storehouse of our mind.

Include past impressions in your mental house cleaning. Stand porter at the door going forward, and do not allow wrong, evil, and fearful thoughts and images enter.

> **"Yesterday is but today's memory,
> and tomorrow is today's dream."**
> *—Khalil Gibran*

Are we making the most out of life?

Life is all around us and inside of us. Through us is the way this invisible Universal energy operates.

You are a vessel for this energy called Life. It is creating through you all the time, every minute. The Universe does not stand still. This power is forming, creating, molding, moving, and expressing every experience in all of our lives.

Take conscious part in this Universal dance, and be one with this life-giving source. Say these powerful words and mean it: "I AM"...because you can!

ANSWER THESE QUESTIONS HONESTLY:

1. What does the Universe consist of? What is its quality?
2. What is your relationship to the Universe?
3. You are a co-creator. Why?
4. Where is life?
5. Can you change your path at any time?
6. Why is the application of truth so important?
7. Are you consciously thinking thoughts of a higher frequency? How does it affect you?
8. Explain why the world is not solid, even though it seems that way.
9. What part does synchronicity play?
10. Are you making the most out of your life?

CHAPTER 15

THE LAWS OF THE UNIVERSE

"Whatever the universal nature assigns to any man at any time is for the good of that man at that time."
—*Marcus Aurelius*

How can you obey the laws of the Universe when you can't obey earthly laws?

Do you still park in the no-parking zone or speed down the highway? Do you make a U-turn when no one is looking? Do you throw trash on the street, cigarette butts out of the car window? Do you have a couple of drinks before you drive? Do you jaywalk?

These examples are simple, every day infractions that everyone is guilty of at one time or another. Nothing is wrong, no big deal, you say. And even though you shouldn't, you continue this behavior.

Do you pay attention to these smaller violations? Do you behave like a good citizen? Are you paying attention to what is right?

"...because you can!"

Make small improvements in these areas, and you will feel better about yourself. Obeying these simple laws will give you self-respect, and gradually you will start to obey the more complex Laws of the Universe. Naturally, you will also start to work with them rather than against them.

By recognizing that you already are part of this greater Universal consciousness, you will flow with it and not against it. You will become one with the current of life.

"The law of harvest is to reap more than you sow. Sow an act, and you reap a habit. Sow a habit and you reap a character. Sow a character and you reap a destiny."
—James Allen

Everyday tests

We are constantly presented with opportunities and challenges that we must address so that we can grow in our spiritual unfoldment. The more we know, the more we have to learn—and the more will be asked of us. The better we want to be, the better we have to become, and we will get away with no less. We no longer slip and slide, making mistakes without being instantly reminded through unpleasant experiences, our wrong thoughts made manifest.

Once you have entered the realm of righteousness, being semi-good is no longer acceptable.

We have to be accurate in our thinking and follow the basic Laws of Nature, the Universe, and constantly adhere to them. These rules and laws have to be properly applied daily, continuously, and with much correctness so they can produce that which we desire.

By obeying the laws, your quality of life will improve.

> **"Our lives are a sum total of the choices we have made."**
> *—Wayne Dyer*

What are some of the Universal Laws?

- The Law of the Allness of Good
- The Law of Cause and Effect
- The Law of Like attracts Like
- The Law of Attraction
- The Law of Individuality
- The Law of Progress in Unfoldment
- The Law of Proportion
- The Law of Relativity
- The Law of Mass Consciousness

> **"Quantum physics thus reveals a basic oneness of the universe."**
> *—Erwin Schrodinger*

Let's take a closer look.

"...because you can!"

The Law of the Allness of Good

The good alone is real. In reality, good is all and so evil must be unreal. Let me explain. Intelligence is good. Wisdom is good. Intelligence and Wisdom cannot be evil as it would be the opposite, which would make Intelligence and Wisdom not intelligent and not wise. It would negate their substance.

Harmony is the underlying principle of all life.

Why bother being good? Why make an effort?

Because, when we look at the world without the man-made evils and destruction, we can see this goodness. We have to restore this visible dimension back to its natural perfection.

You are so accustomed to doubt the Allness of Good that you are not seeing reality. You expect people to be dishonest, careless, and evil. You think they do not have your best interest in mind. But no matter how it looks, you cannot be affected by someone else's thought, unless you allow yourself to believe what someone else says.

"All human beings are interconnected, one with all other elements in creation."
—Henry Reed

Consider this quote by William Shakespeare: "There is nothing either good or bad, just thinking makes it so."

This quote is true and often quoted. It really depends on how you look at things or your sense about things. Consciousness and its activity (thought) being the creator or active force, causes both good and bad. As we have learned, consciousness does not differentiate; it only creates.

Why not give people the benefit of the doubt? See them as good and loving. See them as helpful and kind. They will respond to you. After all, they are a reflection of you, reflecting your sense of them.

In my career I have dealt with many so-called difficult people: entertainment executives, movie stars, famous musicians, and so forth. Many of them were known to be a handful. However, keeping my sense right about the true essence of those characters, I have developed many good relationships and have truly enjoyed working with them.

This, of course, goes for all people. Your nagging aunt or your pesky cousin are good and loving people in reality. It is your sense of them that you experience. They react to your perception of them.

You just have to change your sense about them; it's that simple!

Law of Cause and Effect, in proper order

We break the Law of Cause and Effect by reversing them, giving cause to outside forces: the wind, weather, environment, circumstances, and so forth.

"...because you can!"

We blame everything and everyone instead of looking at ourselves.

If you are suffering from some ill effect, such as sickness or poverty, regardless of the discomfort you manifested, it is because you have violated in some way the Laws of Nature. Ignorance of the Laws and their workings does not excuse you.

It is your purpose, your job, your aim in life to discover for yourself what these Laws are and to live in accordance with them. Trying to get away without doing the work will backfire.

Your conscience knows what must be done. In time of need, when you need it most, you will be able to draw from your understanding, and it will back you up and guide you.

Cause always comes from within and manifests as effect out into the visible world. Cause is invisible and starts in the mental. You are cause for your own experiences as I am cause for mine. We are all causers in this world. We co-created this Universe.

Effect is the visible manifestation of the invisible cause. Effect is only a picture of what has been thought by you and all people on this plane. It is changeable at any time.

As we discovered, our thinking is causative and causes everything we see, hear, touch, and feel. We will discover the importance of keeping our causative thoughts right and good.

> **"All differences in this world are of degree, and not of kind, because oneness is the secret of everything."**
> —*Swami Vivekananda*

Surely you will admit that Universal Love filling the consciousness of each individual will not leave room for fear and hate. It is the only possible way to stop the insanity of crime and war forever. No new punishment will ever deter the criminal, and no new weapon will ever end war as long as the minds of individuals entertain thoughts of crime and greed.

Replace these thoughts of crime and greed with thoughts of truth and goodness. Let love fill the mind of every individual and cast out fear, hate, and dishonesty. You will have a world in which every individual is working together toward the goal of mutual understanding and mutual well-being. This is the true correction using cause and effect in its proper order.

> **"Praying without ceasing is not ritualized, nor are there even words. It is a constant state of awareness of oneness with God."**
> —*Peace Pilgrim*

The news is telling you every day how horrible and awful people behave. Evil appearances are only as real as you believe they are. They only have as much power as you give them. It is not real at all. Again, it is the misuse of cause and effect. Thinking that all is created outside of yourself, without any control over the circumstance, is erroneous.

"...because you can!"

Only Intelligence is real, and Intelligence would not make anything that is less than perfect. All bad or evil-looking things and occurrences are man-made and nothing more than someone's (or your) wrong, distorted, evil, or lesser sense manifested. Always remember the Law works either way; it does NOT differentiate.

It is you who has to differentiate; you are the chooser, the judge, and the executioner. You are the cause, and your world is the effect of your thoughts.

"You and I are essentially infinite choice-makers. In every moment of our existence, we are in that field of all possibilities where we have access to an infinity of choices."
—Deepak Chopra

Law of Like attracts Like

Just as the seeds in the ground bring forth fruit after their kind, your thoughts will do the same. Alike things will spring forth. A pumpkin seed will produce a pumpkin, and a tomato seed will grow into a tomato. The gardener knows what he or she has planted and can expect to harvest what was sown.

So it is with your thoughts. Hateful thoughts will return hate. Loving thoughts will produce love. Kind and generous gestures will return kindness and abundance.

You are the gardener of your life. Plant only the right seeds (thoughts) and water (nurture) them plentiful.

Nourish and love what you plant, and it will grow and multiply. This is the Law of Like attracts Like.

> **"Loving people live in a loving world. Hostile people live in a hostile world. Same world."**
> *—Wayne Dyer*

The Law of Attraction

Your thought frequencies will attract what reflects your state of mind. Your thoughts are like magnets when in action. You attract what you think most of and, therefore, it is necessary to focus when working on a specific desire.

You probably have experienced this phenomenon of driving down the freeway. You just bought a new car, your favorite model and color, and all of a sudden you see this car everywhere. You have tuned in to this specific model and now you are paying attention, or "seeing" it for the first time.

Maybe you desired a specific piece of clothing that you saw at the mall. You've been thinking about it but just didn't want to spend the money. You can feel it and are wearing it in your mind. You are focusing on the enjoyment that this new garment will bring you once you own it. A week later, your friend or partner has a surprise for you. Guess what it is? You attracted this gift. You created it for you, even though it looks like someone else bought it for you.

Visualize in detail to make any wish more real. When you want to attract a certain good, you have to be specific as explained in the Desire chapter.

Of course, it also works the other way around. If you think negatively and send out low thought frequencies, it will attract negativity, unpleasantness, and despair.

So make sure that you emit the positive frequencies that you want to attract. This is the Law of Attraction.

> **"Everyone should be respected as an individual, but no one idolized."**
> *—Albert Einstein*

The Law of Individuality

We are all individuals, yet we are all one. We are individual as to our identity and our abilities and our creative power and freedom of choice.

This basic Law is important in *all* relationships. We must see that everyone has the right to live the way he or she sees fit.

We cannot push our beliefs and wants on other people, even on members of our family. We break this Law constantly. We behave this way not only with family, spouses, and friends, but also with business partners and others we come into contact with.

We cannot look to others for happiness or fulfillment of any kind. We have to find these qualities within ourselves. We cannot judge others or criticize them or tell them what to do; it is their life, their choice.

We can only support others in a loving way. We should not enable them by always doing for them; rather, we should support them by thinking right, good, and loving thoughts about their true nature. Providing these supportive thoughts will not interfere with their right of freedom.

All of us must reach the ultimate state of being in our own time, in our own way, and when we are ready. We are on this plane to work out the simple, first steps of life. Like Kindergarten, we can graduate to the higher grades and learn what is truly important in life, after we have mastered the simpler steps.

Remember, this is only the beginning stage. We have only just awakened. We have only just begun.

We will have to work out our destiny individually, always remembering that in the grand scheme of life, we are all connected and we are all one with regard to substance and quality.

> **"Progress lies not in enhancing what is, but in advancing toward what will be."**
> *—Khalil Gibran*

"...because you can!"

The Law of Progress in Unfoldment

The Law of Progress cannot be broken, only slowed down. We all progress in our daily lives, and we learn something every day.

You can also see the natural progression all over the world. Some areas are slower than others, but there is always progress. You might not recognize it immediately, but Life always goes upward, up in the scale of being.

We as metaphysicians have the duty to focus on our progress and not sit idle in this task. By not applying what we learn, we will experience setbacks and woes. When this happens, we have no one to blame but ourselves.

However, when we feel a sense of progress, we feel happy, strong, satisfied, and invigorated because this is how it's supposed to be.

So focus on the important things in life and keep your priorities straight. Set goals that are right and good for your progress.

Be persistent and do not give up or wander off your path. Insist and know that it can be done, and be determined to achieve whatever you set out to do. Know and feel your desire so you can taste it with all of your being, and it will be yours.

Always look upward; always look for improvement no matter how small. It is a long road but a rewarding one.

> "Keep your face always toward the sunshine—and
> shadows will fall behind you."
> —*Walt Whitman*

Law of Proportion

You can say that your life experience, good or bad, is in exact proportion of your output, good or bad. So what you think will affect your experience in exact proportion to your quality of thought.

Let me say it in so many ways: Your abundance will reflect in exact proportion to your wealth consciousness. Your health will manifest in exact proportion to your healthful thinking. Your happiness will depend on the number of happy thoughts you think.

It takes at least 51 percent of right thoughts to swing the pendulum in your favor. You can think a little better, and your experience will be just a little better. You can think a lot better and turn your life around.

> "I cannot always control what goes on outside. But I
> can always control what goes on inside."
> —*Wayne Dyer*

Law of Relativity

Everything in life is relative to what?

It is relative to our understanding of life. Our understanding is always relative to how we see our

"...because you can!"

environment, the world inside and out, and hence the big picture.

Our everyday happenings are relative to the state of mind we are currently in. Your specific experience is relative to your understanding of the workings of the Laws and the application thereof.

In our quest to achieve perfect Understanding, we rise in the scale of being, steadily and surely. It is certain that you will progress in relative proportion to your becoming more and more aware of the truth of being.

As this is a limitless Universe; its rules exist in many different areas, including mathematics and music. We know there are never-ending digits and numbers and endless musical notes. We can see limitlessness in colors—shades of all kinds. With plants and animals, countless species are proof of this immeasurable abundance.

The above examples are relative to what we see, hear, touch, taste, smell, reason, and understand. They are relative to what we perceive and to what our senses conceive.

Everyone reading this book has a relative sense of what I am saying, reflecting their understanding at this time. This is a relative world, but we are striving to understand the Ultimate.

Don't be fooled; there is always more to understand, even in the Ultimate state of being.

> **"Man is wise and constantly in quest of more wisdom; but the ultimate wisdom, which deals with beginnings, remains locked in a seed. There it lies, the simplest fact of the universe and at the same time the one which calls forth faith rather than reason."**
> **—Hal Borland**

Manifestation of mass belief

Individual thought is, as we know, causative. Collective thought or consciousness is an even greater force. Collective thought is projected into the Universe as mass effect.

When groups of people get together for a specific cause, this combined thinking creates a huge force. It sparks action.

Look at the economy (good or bad), political progress, and, on the opposite side, wars and racism. These are all manifestations of mass belief or collective consciousness and can be made better and corrected by this combined mental force. Do you realize this power?

Good causes and charitable thinking accompanied by action—such as saving the earth from pollution, saving animals from extinction, and feeding the hungry—have all been known to make a great impact.

The original purpose will become more powerful as more thinkers join the cause. Mass thinking will make it so. It will transform the world's perception and ultimately the change will occur.

Unfortunately, many collective thinkers engage in negative causes such as those who protest against people's rights, those who instigate riots, or those who hunt defenseless animals. Protesting against war is not a positive action but marching for peace is. Do you see the point?

"Just as treasures are uncovered from the earth, so virtue appears from good deeds, and wisdom appears from a pure and peaceful mind. To walk safely through the maze of human life, one needs the light of wisdom and the guidance of virtue."
—Buddha

Earthly Laws

Other laws, such as the Law of Gravity, the Law of Physics, Law of Science, and any other laws that we are familiar with, coincide with Universal Laws.

Laws and rules guide us, but Universal Intelligence knows what is best for all of us. It simply wants us to stay out of trouble in order that we may be able to live in peace and harmony with one another.

However, even in ancient times we needed some direction to keep us on track. Consider, for example, the Ten Commandments. These Ten Commandments are good, basic, moral laws that help keep us out of trouble with ourselves, family, friends, and neighbors.

Remember, when these words were written, times were vastly different. But the basic message still applies. Let's look at the real meaning; let's find the basic message.

> **"That deep emotional conviction of the presence of a superior reasoning power, which is revealed in the incomprehensible universe, forms my idea of God."**
> **—*Albert Einstein***

Here are the Ten Commandments and their plain interpretation:

And God spoke all these words, saying:

1. **"I am the Lord your God, who brought you out of the land of Egypt, out of the house of bondage. You shall have no other gods before me."**

There is only one God, namely Universal Intelligence. It is an all-encompassing power. It is all good, all perfect, and all loving. You are part of this substance, and you should not make anything that is outside of yourself (or not in accordance with Universal Law) God or Cause.

If you say "I caught a cold because I sat in a draft," you make the weather God. When you say "My boss makes me do this or that, and I have no control over it," you make your boss God. Any time you say "I am broke because of the economy," you make the government God. This list goes on and on.

"...because you can!"

We have many gods, but remember, "You shall have only one God" and "You shall have no other gods before me." As you are part of this God, you shall not make anything other than yourself cause for you. You shall know the God of Love, Wisdom, and Understanding.

**"The highest revelation is that God is in every man."
—*Ralph* Waldo Emerson**

2. **You shall not make for yourself any carved image, or any likeness of anything that is in heaven above, or that is in the earth beneath, or that is in the water under the earth; you shall not bow down to them nor serve them. For I, the Lord your God, am a jealous God, visiting the iniquity of the fathers on the children to the third and fourth generations of those who hate me, but showing mercy to thousands, to those who love Me and keep My commandments.**

In ancient times, idolatry was very common. These days it has mostly vanished. You can still find it in the churches, though. People pray to statues, crosses, and other items of worship in the hopes of favors from a personal God.

Who are you praying to? Do you think this picture of Jesus has power? The real God does not listen nor does he hear your beseeching. The real God is just and impersonal. He rewards the seekers and shows mercy to the ones that love the Truth and keep the Laws or Universal Commandments.

Right thoughts are real and have power; wrongs thoughts are unreal and have no power. They are mistakes and in need of corrections. Do not blindly believe in organizations, churches, or any kind of cult teaching. Prove the effectiveness to yourself and then decide.

Good results will show you what is right. Get right results through your trust in your own power, and connect with the Divine Guidance that the Universe provides for you. Your mind's convictions will not only change your experience, they will also create a change in your body.

Don't be afraid to assume this position of being part of the Almighty God. Be grateful that you are.

"Each one prays to God according to his own light."
—Mohandas Gandhi

3. You shall not take the name of the Lord your God in vain, for the Lord will not hold him guiltless who takes His name in vain.

Look in the dictionary and see what the word "vain" means. Its description includes words like disrespectful, blasphemous, fruitless, pointless, excessively proud, inflated, arrogant, and conceited.

It is very plain. We should never disrespect the Laws. We should not disrespect Universal Intelligence. We should be humble and grateful for what we have received from this Almighty source. And most of all, we have to respect ourselves and live accordingly.

"...because you can!"

> **"Heaven means to be one with God."**
> **—Confucius**

4. Remember the Sabbath day, to keep it holy. Six days you shall labor and do all your work, but the seventh day is the Sabbath of the Lord your God. In it you shall do no work: you, nor your son, nor your daughter, nor your manservant, nor your maidservant, nor your cattle, nor your stranger who is within your gates. For in six days the Lord made the heavens and the earth, the sea, and all that is in them, and rested the seventh day. Therefore the Lord blessed the Sabbath day and hallowed it.

In Genesis, we read that "God rested on the Sabbath." What it means is that after we have done diligent mental work, thinking our best possible thoughts, we will come to a conclusion about the desired yearning.

The six days of (mental) labor symbolize our senses.

Our five senses (days) are hear, see, touch, feel, taste, and the sixth sense (day) is reason. The seventh day (Sabbath) is the culmination of the six senses, which we call Understanding. In this state of Understanding (the Sabbath), our mind will experience rest.

To clarify, the conclusion or understanding we gain after diligent reasoning about what we hear, see, touch, taste, smell, and feel will manifest our desire and, therefore, give us mental rest. We will no longer have to labor. We rest on the seventh day.

> **"As we move into the 21st century, there's what the Bible calls a 'quickening of the spirit'."**
> **—Neale Donald Walsch**

5. Honor your father and your mother, that your days may be long upon the land which the Lord your God is giving you.

The "father" represents the male element and the "mother" represents the female element in Mind. We are composed of both elements.

The significance of this statement is that you need both elements to produce in the visible as well as in the mental, or invisible.

The male element is also the reasoning element, and the female element represents the feeling element. You have to honor your reasoning, meaning you have to keep your reasoning on the right side and you have to honor your feelings, keeping them good and loving at all times.

Do not deviate from honoring your mental father and mother.

> **"We need to find God, and he cannot be found in noise and restlessness. God is the friend of silence. See how nature—trees, flowers, grass—grows in silence; see the stars, the moon and the sun, how they move in silence...We need silence to be able to touch souls."**
> **—Mother Teresa**

6. You shall not murder.

This seems obvious when interpreted from a human standpoint. However, it is much deeper than that. By believing that you can take life from another, you are committing not just another sin. You believe that life can be taken away. You believe in the reality of death.

You cannot take life. Life lives.

So as long as you "murder" or believe that you can take life, you are aeons away from entering the kingdom of heaven. You are lost in material confusion. You are dead in the worldly sense.

"Each one prays to God according to his own light."
—*Mohandas Gandhi*

7. You shall not commit adultery.

The true union of the male and female elements are in mind. The so-called physical marriage is only the reflection of this idea projected. Just like giving birth to children, it is the visible effect of giving birth to new ideas in the mental.

You have to stay true to your ideas. The female and the male elements have to be in agreement; knowing and feeling have to unite in consciousness in order to produce. Knowing and feeling have to be one. This is true marriage in heaven, your natural mental state.

Adultery is the straying away from this union. It is straying away from the truth. When you do so, you will lose your way and will not experience the harmony you are searching for.

> **"Truth is the property of no individual but is the treasure of all men."**
> —*Ralph Waldo Emerson*

8. You shall not steal.

There is enough for everyone in this Universe. By thinking you have to take or steal from another, you believe that there is not enough for you. You assume that some are better off and that you received the short end of the stick. You accept the lie that poverty is real and that you are doomed to live a less abundant life.

Taking from another shows disregard for others. It is selfish, egotistical, and cruel. It will leave you with a sense of low self-esteem and guilt.

You might think you can take material things away from the other, but you cannot take mental qualities from them.

When we experience criminal activities or see others being affected by those dishonest ones, we should not have to think of revenge. We should not wish misfortune and punishment. We are not the judge and the jury. The Law will take care of it in its own good time.

"...because you can!"

> **"I'm going to let God be the judge of who goes to heaven and hell."**
> *—Joel Osteen*

9. You shall not bear false witness against your neighbor.

Lying is another sin we are all too familiar with. Lies are simply unacceptable.

But what about the smaller ones, the ones we call white lies? We have all kinds of excuses why it's okay to not always tell the truth.

I am not saying you should be cruel. I am saying you should think about your general honesty when dealing with people. Your neighbor is part of you. In reality, he or she is as good and perfect as you are. You need to accept this fact and act accordingly.

What about lying to yourself?

Are you always truthful when looking at your life? Do you subconsciously hide certain character traits from yourself? Do you see the pettiness you might exhibit, but explain away, saying you are only trying to do things right? Do you see the jealousy arising in your mind, justifying it to yourself, that it's okay to feel this way because someone else has acted a certain way?

Do you tell your children small fibs because you want them to behave? Do you call your employer telling him or her you are sick when you really just want a day to yourself?

All of these hidden untruths have to be brought to light in order to heal.

"God helps those who help themselves."
—Benjamin Franklin

10. You shall not covet your neighbor's house; you shall not covet your neighbor's wife, nor his manservant, nor his maidservant, nor his ox, nor his donkey, nor anything that is your neighbor's."

You are self sufficient, self reliant, self providing and fully competent. You need nothing from anyone. You do not need to want someone else's belongings; you should only long for your own good, already established in yourself.

Life is simple and so are the Laws

When you really think about it, life is simple. The Laws only require you to follow the basic rules. Be good, honest, courageous, loving, and know the power that you inherited. Everything else will follow and fall into place naturally.

This is the way of the Universe, so follow this path… because you can!

"Do not dwell in the past, do not dream of the future, concentrate the mind on the present moment."
—Buddha

ANSWER THESE QUESTIONS HONESTLY:

1. Do you obey earthly Laws, including the smaller ones?
2. Name some of the Universal Laws. Do you live in accordance to those Laws?
3. How do you break the Law of Cause and Effect? Give examples.
4. Do you want to be and live good? What can you do to improve?
5. Do you realize the power of collective or mass consciousness?
6. Are you always honest with yourself and others?
7. Do you subconsciously hide certain character traits from yourself?
8. Do you see yourself as self-sufficient, self-reliant and fully competent?
9. What is your best sense of God, Universal Intelligence?
10. Write down your plan for following the Laws. What will you improve?

CHAPTER 16

CONSCIOUSNESS

"Just as a candle cannot burn without fire, men cannot live without a spiritual life."
—Buddha

There is nothing mysterious about the inner power; there is nothing secret about Consciousness

Let me state it in so many ways: Consciousness is what you are. It is what we all are. It is all there is. All is Consciousness and Consciousness is all.

Robert Scheinfeld, published in 2010, said it perfectly this way:

"When we talk about 'spiritual consciousness' we are talking about a state of Being where all limiting, conflicting and contradictory ideas, thoughts, feelings, beliefs, circumstances and events blend together and dissolve into harmony."

"...because you can!"

Consciousness is power, and this power is "you." It is your substance. And since it is also active and not just a latent power, it is here for you to use.

Collective consciousness is what we call "we, the people."

We are both teachers and students. It works both ways: we attract each other so that we can learn from the experiences and character of the other. We reflect each other and through this reflection see lessons that need attention.

We are masters but we are also servants. We are individuals, yet one. When we look at the other, we really look at ourselves.

Have you ever noticed that when you need to learn a specific lesson, or you are searching for an answer to a problem, someone will come into your life that is able to help provide an answer?

Many times after the situation has cleared and you received your answer, this person moves on and disappears out of your life, just as he or she entered it seemingly out of the blue.

Consciousness works seamlessly and constantly.

"There is a supreme power and ruling force which pervades and rules the boundless Universe. You are part of this power."
—Prentice Mulford

Consciousness was and always will be

Consciousness wasn't born and will not die. It always was and it always will be.

The visible Universe was supposedly born at the time of the Big Bang. However,

Consciousness gave birth to this visible Universe. It is the mother and father of all life.

We, as individual particles of consciousness, are slowly awakening to the facts of life, and we are becoming more conscious of our being. We are gradually glimpsing Universal unfoldment, looking at and reflecting upon the whole picture, which is incomprehensible as it is unlimited. It cannot be understood all at once, or it would be limited or finite.

We are a conscious participant in this unfolding process of the Universe.

Consciousness manifests itself through visible forms in this world, but all forms are still mental in nature. They become seemingly solid to be usable on this plane of existence. When form dissolves, it goes back to its essence, which is energy, not matter.

It is necessary for humanity to awaken to these facts. Each of us can be a leader and teacher in this movement toward the light. It has begun, and we are well on our way to greater understanding.

"...because you can!"

Again, you are this substance called Consciousness, and its power flows through you. It inspires you and guides you. You can use this newly acquired knowledge for the greater good.

Choose deliberately and knowingly to be part of this Universal awakening, and be part of its life-changing purpose.

> **"If you want to find the secrets of the Universe, think in terms of energy, frequency and vibration."**
> **—*Nikola Tesla***

Anything you do has a purpose

Each of us is an integral part of collective consciousness, and each of us has a specific purpose. What this purpose is needs to be discovered. The general purpose of life is, as I pointed out in an earlier chapter, for you to learn your daily lessons and to enjoy the process. Learn how to think more positively, lovingly, abundantly, and gain a healthy consciousness. Enjoy the challenges that come along every day, and know they will help you to gain more understanding. Looking at the tribulation in the correct way by seeing it as a stepping stone to further your enlightenment will surely make it more attractive to you. It will become a help-mate rather then a negative experience.

So your specific purpose is to find out what your life's lessons are. What path shall you take? Why are you here? And how you can make these lessons enjoyable? Remember that enjoyment is the ultimate experience on this plane.

You have to discover your talents and find what makes you happy. What makes you fulfilled?

It includes exploring your abilities and the gifts you possess that can contribute to the world. How can you be of service, and how you can help others make their lives better?

This ability and willingness to share your talents will in turn bestow upon you happiness and satisfaction.

"Everyone has been made for some particular work, and the desire for that work has been put in every heart."
—*Rumi*

Seek and ye shall find

At some point along this journey, we will no longer have to seek who we are and where we came from. The answers will come in due time. We will know the truth, and we will be one with the Almighty source. However, do not be mistaken; we keep our individuality. We will always maintain our identity.

We'll realize that we have been part of this source all along. Through this transition, from searching to understanding, we will think and act from a higher dimension, right here and now. We will solve all of our problems with this newfound awareness.

"...because you can!"

To reiterate, anything you do has a purpose. Focus on your purpose with good intentions and clear awareness. Do everything you do for enjoyment, as enjoyment is your true purpose. So if you don't like what you are doing right now, accept it graciously and do the best you can without resentment and spite until you have changed the circumstances.

During this period, which will teach you patience and endurance, you can think, imagine, and create your new world and act on it. You are the creator.

"Every moment of your life is infinitely creative and the Universe is endlessly bountiful. Just put forth a clear enough request, and everything your heart desires must come to you."
—Shakti Gawain

Don't wait to start living

Don't wait until you think the time has come. That is, don't wait until you retire, until the kids are out of the house, until you have more money, and it's less busy at work. Don't put it in the future. Start living now.

Paint yourself a big, wonderful picture of happiness, and then embrace it and tackle it piece by piece. And, like a puzzle, the picture will come together and look beautiful.

Many people only exist; they do not live. Existing is drudgery, but living is joy. Merely getting through the day is wasted time, and experiencing the day is delightful.

Blessed is the man or woman that can find ecstasy in mere living!

"The key to growth is the introduction of higher dimensions of consciousness into our awareness."
—Lao Tzu

Slow down

Most people have the "busy syndrome," always running around doing something. Keep a record of what you do on a daily basis and note how many unimportant items you have on this list. How many chores can you delete and replace with valuable time, or things you really want to do?

Empower your life with creative action; become who you want to be. Clear your Consciousness of unnecessary debris.

Keep your Consciousness free of clutter and experience your true self now.

Karen's story

The Long Ride Home

It used to be that my ride home was just me, belted in, music playing, windows rolled down and sounds of the city as background while I replayed the day, thought about the future and crawled through the present in bumper to bumper traffic.

I thought about that tonight as I placed my Bluetooth in my ear and dialed up person after person in a futile attempt to fill the time with conversation as I made my long drive home. I listened to my music, which is very important to me, only this time, without the distraction of conversation in my ear, I really listened to the music. And I listened to my thoughts, and how the music affected me, and realized the Bluetooth had to go. I missed alone time in my car. I hadn't realized how vital it was, until I let myself really tune in to ME with my own thoughts and my own feelings. It was liberating.

The information superhighways allow us to multitask and absorb all that we can for as long as we can take it, and, silly us, sometimes we don't know when enough is enough. Tonight I felt my threshold. I want to live in the moment, not document it with continual Facebook updates noting my every move and thought. If I go see a concert, I don't want to be the first person to download a video clip of it on YouTube—I want to hear the musician, feel his words, and have the consummate experience of BEING there in body and mind.

It is vital we create alone time with ourselves—grab it, carve it out of our million + one things To-Do list and really listen to ourselves. In reality, we don't need to speed up or ramp anything up one more notch. We won't fall behind, I guarantee it.

Because when we listen to our spirit, when we allow ourselves the precious time to get to know the real us, then there is no time. It becomes the enjoyment of the moment. It allows enlightenment. It is the eternal moment. And, as I discovered tonight, it will be the best ride home.

"Thou wilt find rest from vain fancies if thou doest every act in life as though it were thy last."
—Aristotle

Weed out the unnecessary daily business. Take the time to create your ideal environment. Have a vision and goal and work toward implementing that goal in a calm state of mind. Stay focused without strain. Keep your enthusiasm high without anxiety.

Your energy field will change. You will live and have your being on a higher frequency.

Ralph Waldo Emerson once said, "Nothing great has ever been achieved without enthusiasm." A true statement, indeed, and we surely give more when we are excited and interested in what we are doing.

Remember, each of us is an integral part of collective consciousness. Each of us has a purpose that fits within the Universal picture. We are all a piece of the cosmic puzzle.

"Be careful of your moods and feelings, for there is an unbroken connection between your feelings and your visible world."
—Neville Goddard

"...because you can!"

Your Consciousness has the ability to think

You think, reason, and feel. Your thoughts are composed of all kinds of past impressions, experiences, criticisms, fears, and new ideas collected along the way with wistful expectations.

When thoughts come to mind, you reason about them and a certain feeling will accompany the reasoning process. Your moods and dispositions all have a hand in the outcome of your desires in the visible world.

When you hear about unpleasant stories in the media, make sure that you remember the following:

You are not the judge and the jury

Always remember that it is not up to you to judge people and prescribe punishment. You are not the judge and the jury. Nature will take care of that.

There will always be a mental effect for wrong doing. No one can escape the penalty, no matter how long it takes. Nature, the Universe, governs all wisely and well at all times. You can call it Karma or anything you'd like. The fact is that you will receive in exact proportion to your mental output. This goes for everyone; no one is exempt from this Universal Law.

> **"Nothing in the affairs of men is worthy of great anxiety."**
> *—Plato*

Negativity is a disease

Negativity is uneasy and disquieting thinking. Negativity draws negative people to you. The Law of Attraction applies; it goes both ways.

Nagging and complaining because nothing is ever good enough and gossip and hurtful behavior are on many people's everyday schedule. This is not living; this is vegetating. It's a waste of Life.

Life is a treasure, something you cherish, and your duty is to value this Life you have been given. It is a privilege to be part of this Universal perfect Consciousness. You should honor your Life.

"As your faith is strengthened you will find that there is no longer the need to have a sense of control, that things will flow as they will, and that you will flow with them, to your great delight and benefit."
—*Wingate Paine*

You think you have control

In this world, control is a major factor to many people. Businesses and work environments are controlled by upper management and business owners. Politics and world economics are controlled by politicians and economic leaders. Even families are controlled by certain members. You control your children. Or do you?

Control over others is not a good idea because it takes away the God-given ability to choose and limits the individual's self-sufficiency. Yes, we need rules and guidelines. But control is an extreme form of diminishing other people's power.

Having been an executive in the corporate world, I understand that someone has to be in charge. This means the department leader needs to sustain control over employees, suppliers, and sub-contractors or else the workplace becomes chaos. It is the manner in which control is delegated that matters. Being in charge does not mean being controlling.

When you realize that you are in charge of your own life, your need to control others will diminish. You will allow others to be themselves and make decisions. You will be more trusting.

When you reach a higher level of understanding, you will even allow yourself to be free of controlling yourself.

Look at the illusion of control. How many corporate executives, no matter how much control they believe they have, foresaw the possible collapse of Greece or the damage incurred by Hurricane Katrina or the electrical blackout that left parts of Arizona, Mexico, and California without power for more than twenty-four hours?

In today's digital world, power dissolves quickly. Those spiritually prepared will survive. They will always know how to sustain themselves. They will always find a way to revitalize their individual world and they will play a positive part in the collective world.

When you let go of this imaginary control, you will happily give yourself to the Universe and trust in the

Allness of Good. You will understand that Life wants you to succeed and, with this perfect trust, everything will merge together seamlessly. All will be just right, flawless, and wonderful.

> **"No problem can be solved from the same level of consciousness that created it."**
> *—Albert Einstein*

How congested thinking reflects in this world

Today's major pollution symbolizes *congested* thinking in the mental.

Let me explain:

Pollution is the introduction of contaminants into a natural environment. Air pollution is the release of chemicals and particulates into the atmosphere. It looks like we pollute the air with common gaseous pollutants, to include carbon monoxide, sulfur dioxide, chlorofluorocarbons, and so on. You will say that pollution comes from cars, factories, and other man-made sources. This is your "now" sense that you were taught.

The oceans are polluted with human waste and carelessly disposed of trash. We all know the stories. As the population grows in the cities, we experience more pollution in those areas. Country folks living a simpler life tend to be less congested in their thinking, so they experience less pollution.

I am telling you that pollution comes from polluted thinking: a lack of love and concern for the planet.

"...because you can!"

Greed is a key element, being selfish in wanting what you want without considering the natural beauty of this mental and physical world.

However, the truth remains the same. Pollution is also mental.

Limited thinking, polluted with a material sense and not true spiritual awareness, is the cause. In this world a lot seems evil, and this belief causes polluted thinking. We must make sure that we do not assign power to something that doesn't exist. Evil is not real; it is man-made and will vanish when we realize that the path to heaven is the only reality. Harmony rules!

When your priority becomes peace and happiness, you are on your way to spiritual joy.

Keep at it and help others to see the light, nudging them gently toward a better Earth. We have been chosen to live at the same time, going through similar experiences. Remember, even though we are individuals, we are also all one, concluding that love is the common denominator.

"The world is a meaningful place, where everyone is working out their own life's purpose."
—*Deepak Choprah*

Yes, it is your responsibility to search, learn, better yourself, and gain an Understanding of the Truth. Find out for yourself what pure consciousness consists of... because you can!

ANSWER THESE QUESTIONS HONESTLY:

1. What is consciousness and how do you use it?
2. What is the ultimate experience on this plane?
3. We are teachers and students at the same time. How can you apply this knowledge?
4. What are your talents and what makes you fulfilled?
5. What is your vision for your future?
6. Do you have the busy syndrome?
7. What can you eliminate from your schedule?
8. Pollution: Can you see the connection to mental congestion?
9. When your priority becomes peace and joy, what happens?
10. Write down the difference between your consciousness and collective consciousness.

CHAPTER 17

SENSE

What am I? What is my highest mental concept of myself? What is my sense of myself?

> *"I think and that is all that I am."*
> *—Wayne Dyer*

I am the "I AM." The "I AM" is all there is in my world. I am the thinker and the causer. Consciousness or Perfect Intelligence, the Universal source or cause of all, is the substance of which I am made.

Given the ability to reason, choose, judge, and cause, it is up to me to unfold the inherent perfection of what I am by nature. I have the ability to understand, and I have the ability to sense. All I can do in reality is sense all there is, including others.

All of the above applies to you and everyone else. But I wanted you to read it out aloud, saying "I AM" over and over again, so you can hear the impact this statement has on your sense of self.

"...because you can!"

Intelligence is mental and so is my sense of everything I comprehend. Intelligence is good and Goodness is intelligent, or it wouldn't be good. I am here on this plane to test concepts and so are YOU.

When we talk about *sense* in this chapter, we are not only talking about the word in the usual way, as in hear, see, touch, taste, or smell. We are talking about your "sense of" in a spiritual way.

To sense something spiritually means that we give recognition to the truth about anything in the mental. You can sense right or wrong, but it is your sense of what you are sensing that gives it its quality.

It is up to you to determine whether it's good or bad. Remember the Shakespeare quote: "There is nothing good or bad, just thinking makes it so."

You are sensing all the time. You are sensing yourself well or sick, happy or sad, wealthy or poor.

"Sense is purely mental and in the last analysis, life itself is nothing but sense."
—*William W. Walter*

How is your Character?

Everybody claims to want a better life, but few make the effort to really work on the unfoldment and necessary purification of the Soul.

Individual tests have to be solved and challenges overcome before comprehension of the truth can be accomplished. Put importance on your progress, and always take quality before quantity. A positive, quality thought will go a long way toward advancing balance and harmony in your life.

Observe your character. Is it pleasant, joyful, and loving? Are you by nature kind, playful, and giving? Or is your character filled with stubbornness and judgment? Are you opinionated and spiteful—or worse, dishonest and biased? Harsh questions, I know, but they need to be considered. They need to be answered.

It is essential to develop a good quality of character. Continue to empty out all previous concepts and be willing to refrain from temptation to take the easy route and revert to the old habits.

The process is arduous. You will be climbing a steep mountain and not coasting along an easy route. It takes on-going effort and self-evaluation to change your character, but you will find freedom, greater self-sufficiency, and greater self- confidence.

In order to fully succeed, you have to have a good heart and be strictly honest. I truly believe that everyone who reads these pages has already taken the first steps to self-improvement. You are already good; you are just working on making yourself even better.

Don't shy away from the goal. Embrace the corrections you make in yourself. Do not be dependant on anyone or anything. Look out for your own best interest first, but be fair to others. You cannot take care of anyone unless you take care of yourself first.

As mentioned before, be compassionate and caring, but don't get involved in other people's affairs. Sense them as perfect beings; they are of the same substance as you are.

> **"Character is higher than intellect. A great soul will be strong to live as well as think."**
> **—*Ralph Waldo Emerson***

Keep the best sense you can about everything

William W. Walter said in one of his great papers to "never repeat, hear or see any kind of imperfection. See only the beautiful and good, even in the unlovely and unkind."

I know on this plane it seems difficult and sometimes impossible, but you can make a concerted effort to focus on what is right. Eventually, you will see your world improve. As your sense changes, so will your surroundings. In previous chapters I pointed out that improved thinking will change your world. Let me take it up a notch. I am saying that not only your *thought of,* but also your *sense of* has to improve.

Repeat at all times and under all circumstances: "The good alone is all." It should be your daily mantra. I see perfect cause and perfect effect at all times.

Knowing that you are the cause, you can produce the perfect effect.

Very early in my studies, I walked home from work after having spent the day at the box office of a popular music nightclub on Sunset Boulevard. I had collected my paycheck, cashed it, and happily entered my house. Shorty thereafter, I heard a knock at the door.

Innocently, I opened it, and asked the stranger, "How can I help you?" Pointing a gun barrel at me, he said, "You can help me by giving me all your money."

I had to undress and lay down on the bed, closing my eyes as he went through my closets and handbags, finding my hard-earned money.

I had only studied metaphysics for about a year at that time. I didn't know much about the power of thought, but I had learned one phrase in class, which is the phrase below:

"It's good, nothing but good, and nothing than good can come to me, it's in my mentality."
—*William W. Walter*

As I lay there, still seeing the gun in my mind, I repeated this phrase over and over again in my mind. I believed it with all of my heart. I knew it was the truth. It saved my life.

I heard the door close and he was gone. No harm was done to me, and the little money he found didn't

"...because you can!"

matter much to me, knowing that this Goodness I trusted at that time would provide for me again.

I have come a long way since then. Thirty years later, I know that I know, that I know. The Allness of Good is everywhere; all is good!

"Today is a new day and I promise myself to let go of yesterday. I will live this day to the fullest and best of my abilities."
—Ulrike

Always keep your highest ideal in mind

Don't waver in your decisions. Do not be deterred. If you have fallen, get back up on that horse, and ride it. Practice makes perfect. Keep your highest sense in all that you do. Movement should always inch forward.

We must refuse the imperfections we see in others, in our surroundings, and in the world, as well as in ourselves. We must watch our thoughts all the time no matter what the appearance, and we must maintain high standards.

However, don't beat yourself up and judge yourself harshly if you've lowered your sense about something. Just go right back to the truth, and correct your mental mistake. All mistakes are only mental mistakes, and they need to be corrected in your mentality.

> **"Such as are your habitual thoughts, such also will be the character of your mind; for the soul is dyed by the thoughts."**
> *—Marcus Aurelius*

Look at your life. Reflect.

Looking at your life will give you a certain sense about it; it will trigger different feelings and emotions. Each of us has a different sense about any given situation, even when looked at exactly at the same time. We all sense each other differently. We sense our environments differently. Studies show that we even sense colors in different shades.

You have your own individual sense. There is no one like you.

It is really your own viewpoint of people, experiences, and events that started during your upbringing, your teachings, and your current beliefs. Some things that look big to you might be small potatoes to another and vice versa. Something might really make you angry and trigger a certain unpleasant feeling within you, while someone else just laughs it off. Something that you find delightful and entertaining might be thought of as a waste of time by someone else.

> **"An eye for an eye only ends up making the whole world blind."**
> *—Mohandas Gandhi*

"...because you can!"

Always take a step back before you react. Observe and look at the reality of things. What is really important? What is real? Was it just someone's opinion? What was the truth about it?

After a deep breath, you will see that if you stop taking everything so personally, it loses its punch. Angering events and circumstances lose their impact on you.

During the observation and transition in your life, don't jump to hasty judgments. Strive to be patient and even-tempered. Avoid jumping to conclusions. The result will be a rewarding inner peace.

It's not worth it to fight against silly, unimportant things that really are just someone else's dispositions. Don't allow others to affect you. We cannot control people or events, but we can control how we think about them. We decide how we sense them. It is up to us to make this choice.

Stay with the truth, stay with the pure, and stay with the good and your loving sense. If these pure, loving feelings are buried deep inside of you, let them out. I know you have them; resurrect them today.

This is all about your life.

> "There has never been a time when you and I and the kings gathered here have not existed, not will there be a time when we will cease to exist. As the same person inhabits the body through childhood, youth, and old age, so too at the time of death, he attains another body. The wise are not deluded by these changes."
> —*Bhagarad Gita*

A deeper meaning

What we see in what we call plant life, animals, or people are only visible symbols. It is the way we interpret all life during our relative unfoldment. We still see all and everything in the world, including living beings, as solid.

Everything we observe has a deeper meaning in the invisible. Everything now is therefore our relative sense of what we see. As we progress in our unfoldment, we recognize the true meaning and see it for what it really is. This sounds difficult, but we will keep it practical.

Sooner or later you have to drop the false sense of happiness found in materialism and find your true value within. As you work out the problems of life on this plane, do not become discouraged.

When you have solved one problem and another one shows up, it is only because you are ready to tackle another challenge. It is the way of learning and proving to yourself that all life is mental. You are working out your own salvation in your own time.

Practice makes perfect, as the saying goes, so be patient and diligent, and enjoy even your greatest tribulations. The Law of Progress will make sure that your path continues upward and that you are one step closer to your goal.

> **"Love and doubt have never been on speaking terms."**
> **—Khalil Gibran**

Discouragement and doubt

Let me say this: discouragement and doubt are two of the biggest deterrents in all aspects of life. You are ready to tackle a new passion, change jobs, get married, move to a new city, or attempt a longed-for project or life improvement. You think you are ready to embrace your desire, and slowly doubt comes creeping in.

Am I ready? Can I do this? Will I fail? I've tried this before and it didn't go as well as I expected. The project didn't turn out as I'd hoped. All these doubts open up the door to discouragement.

Do not be discouraged by any failure you experienced in the past, and do not be disheartened by being less successful than you expected. And never doubt yourself and your abilities.

Perhaps you have to take a different approach or better educate yourself or be better prepared for unexpected issues and obstacles, but you can do anything you want to do if you want it strongly enough.

If your desire is not just wishful thinking but intense, so intense that it takes you over and consumes you, your focus will be clear and determined. This is the key to reaching your goal.

The little mental mistakes you make during the day do not just go away. If not addressed, they stay in your consciousness, even when tucked away into your subconscious.

Just like in math, an error will be carried forth in the equation, and so will your wrong thought be carried forth in your experience. Your poor sense will also prevent you from achieving your goals.

Go back and correct the problem so your issues will be solved. Change your sense from failure to success. You have to turn your sense of discouragement into courage.

You can get rid of all of your baggage, hatred, self-pity, envy, malice, and so on, *but* if you still doubt yourself and are discouraged by the slightest mishaps, you will still experience difficulty in manifesting success.

By changing your sense to a more loving attitude, you will have a calmer and more peaceful life; but you will still struggle with your abundance unless your sense changes to a sense of mental wealth.

"...because you can!"

Your sense of courage has to be put in place to eradicate discouragement. You are courage, and you are success!

"It is very important to generate a good attitude, a good heart, as much as possible. From this, happiness in both the short term and the long term for both yourself and others will come."
—*Dalai Lama*

Love yourself and be grateful for all you have accomplished so far

Know that there is more and more waiting for you. Wake up with a sense of gratitude, and give thanks every day for how far you have come. Feel blessed from the time you get up in the morning until you fall asleep. You can rest assured that you have done the right thing; you have acted kindly and you are at peace.

Have you ever asked yourself why you are thinking wrong and sick thoughts?

You are working to keep your thoughts good, prosperous, and wholesome, yet here they are: envy, criticism, self-pity—all of those useless thoughts stemming from previous beliefs, habits, and misunderstandings.

As pointed out numerous times, since birth we have been taught wrong in all aspects of life. We have interpreted the happenings around us according to our sense at the time, with limited understanding. As children we could sense our mother's disapproval. We assumed that she would stop loving us if we continued to upset her. We sensed the love when she fed us, and we associated food with love. We sensed that daddy was near and felt abandoned when he walked out of the room. We didn't know any better.

We have been taught that we are material beings, that we have a material body, that bad things are just as real as good things, and so on—all lies.

Now that we are mature, we must let go of these feelings and temptations. But the road is long. We didn't accumulate these untruths in one day. It took years and will take an investment in time to rearrange our thinking. It will take time to get in the habit of right thought every time. And correcting our thinking is not all it takes; we also have to change our sense about everything that is less than good and perfect.

When those pesky thoughts creep up, say strongly, "No, I will not think like this ever again," "Stop, this is not who I am now," and "No, I will not believe this is real."

Don't dwell on it. Just put your foot down.

> **"Don't limit a child to your own learning,
> for he was born in another time."
> —Rabindranath Tagore**

The way out of trouble is to stop giving it recognition

"...because you can!"

There is nothing you have to be afraid of. There is nothing that you need protection from. Live a good life and stop looking at the woes of the world. You can make a difference by being the best you can be in *your* world. It will multiply.

Love everything and everyone that you come in touch with. Cherish what you have, and give thanks for your blessings. And for crying out loud, stop looking at the wrong side of life!

Instead, say, "I love to think that all is good" or "Only the good is real, and I know it." Then, sense and feel peace and know that you know it.

> **"I will not march against the war,
> but I will march for peace."**
> **—*Mother Teresa***

Yes, Mother Teresa was right. This is what we need to do. We need to focus on peace and goodness—not on war and destruction. We cannot change the war. We can only change our immediate environment. We can send out our healing vibrations that will surely reach their goal. We can contribute to lessen the war by spending our energy on Peace and Love.

> **"All historical experience demonstrates the following: Our earth cannot be changed unless in the not too distant future an alteration in the consciousness of individuals is achieved."**
> **—*Hans Kung***

Practice your sensing skills

In practicing your sensing skills, you can start with a simple exercise, making every day plants grow and flourish. You can talk to them, love them, nourish them, and the more attention you give them, the more they will grow. Plants will respond to your sense of love and caring. But plants cannot talk back to you; they can only respond to our sense as we are the highest life form on this plane.

We all know the incredible connections some humans have to animals and vice versa. Animals will sense your character and you, in turn, can understand their language if you'll just listen. We have dominion over all lower life forms.

As your sense of self improves, your persona will change to reflect this newfound, better sense. You have to sense yourself (and strongly feel) as happy, healthy, and successful as you want to be. You have to sense joy, well-being, and abundance. You do not merely wish it.

Wishful thinking alone does not create. You have to act and apply what you know. You have to desire it with all of your heart and see yourself as already having it.

To complete the picture, your sense of others also has to improve. See others as kind, generous, friendly, and helpful, and send the good and loving thoughts in support of their unfoldment. They are on the same path as you, maybe a step behind or in front of you, but on the same path.

> **"Take praise and bitter persecution
> with the same equanimity of disposition."**
> *—William W. Walter*

You might think that others have disappointed you or treated you unfairly, but by holding those negative feelings, you lower your frequency. You negate your positive sense and are only hurting yourself.

Unless you approve of yourself and respect yourself, the approval from anyone else is of no value. Take the personal feelings out of it. Make it impersonal. You can trust your own nature to show you what needs to be done.

Wrong feeling or sensing weakens you because it robs you of the power to create the best for yourself.

So crawl out of your dark basement, and go to the sunny porch of your mental house. Breathe in the fresh and joyous side of life…because you can!

ANSWER THESE QUESTIONS HONESTLY:

1. Explain your understanding of the word "sense." What does it mean?
2. What is your sense of yourself?
3. What is your highest mental concept of yourself?
4. Has doubt stopped you in reaching your desires?
5. Are you afraid of failure? Why?
6. Do you have faith in the Allness of Good?
7. Can you change your sense about a person you find unpleasant or mean?
8. Are you the best you can be in your world?
9. Are you sensing others as pleasant and good?
10. Practice your sensing skills on plants and animals.

CHAPTER 18

YOUR WORLD, INSIDE AND OUT

Meister Eckhart, a thirteenth-century Catholic monk and scholar, put it this way:

"God created all things in such a way that they are not outside himself, as ignorant people falsely imagine. Rather, all creatures flow outward, but nonetheless remain within God."
—*Meister Eckhart*

God, Universal Intelligence, created all things from within. They are not created from nor are they of the material world. All creatures and things stem from this godly source and are projected out into the visible world. However, the substance of you, us, and all things remain of Universal Intelligence and are of mental origin.

In my world, there is only me and my sense of me. In your world, there is only you and your sense of you.

"...because you can!"

No one knows how you feel and what you think deep down in your heart, not even your family or closest friends. Your feelings, emotions, and thoughts are your own; they are your secret.

Your perception of yourself

Don't see yourself as being a man or woman. Don't buy into being black or white, or whatever color your skin exhibits. Do not think that your sexual orientation is who you are. Do not use the country of your birth as your identity.

All of these are only perceptions. They label you to act one way or another. See yourself as a mentality, a soul. Free yourself of the sense of racial, cultural, and sexual limitation. Act as the free Spirit you are. Your soul does not have a specific color or race; it is not only a man or a woman. It contains all.

**"Every one rushes elsewhere and into the future, because no one wants to face one's own inner self."
—Michel de Montaigne**

Look within your world and not without. Everything you see without is a mere picture of your innermost thoughts and feelings, your sense of. It is a reflection of your soul.

Your world within always shapes your world without, so concentrate on how you really want your world to look. Create a mental picture of your ideal situation.

See what you've already accomplished, and fill yourself with excitement of things yet to come.

You can think anything you'd like, but you have to come to a conclusion in order to express or manifest your desires. It takes both knowing and feeling to bring your ideas into the visible world.

Ask yourself, "What makes me happy, fulfilled, content, empowered, and strong?" "What am I thinking most of during the day?" "Are those thoughts valuable, exhilarating, and encouraging?"

Or, are you negating your positive thoughts by buying into the words you hear spoken by your friends, family, and work associates? Are you wishing for the good and then doubting that you are the all-power shaping your world?

There is a constant flow of more "good" coming into your experience, if you'll allow this stream of Universal goodness to enter your mind.

As your thoughts change, so do the forms and your relationships. Everything in your world corresponds to your vision. Thoughts are things. Things are "thinks."

Keep your attitude right no matter what. Keep your thoughts strong and on the right side!

"Very little is needed to make a happy life; it is all within yourself, in your way of thinking."
—Marcus Aurelius

"...because you can!"

What makes you uncomfortable and why?

Are certain thoughts uncomfortable to you? Is there a subject you'd rather not address? Is there an area in your life that you've swept under the rug and don't want to clean because you think it will be too painful?

Are you neglecting to see the good in everything? Are you selfish and needy? Are you impatient, wanting everything without due process? Are you opinionated and critical?

What would improve the quality of your life? How can you change this?

There are many, many areas in our thinking that have been contaminated by old beliefs and wrong moods. In your journey to betterment, we will experience some problems, or "lesser" reflections. They are leftovers from past, limited thinking. They are not "real"; they are just shadows of past thoughts.

You can change those negative thoughts and emotions by slowly examining every thought and turning it into a positive one. Now that you have awakened, stick with your newfound way of thinking, and soon you will see the improvements. You will start noticing small changes for the better in exact accordance to your changed thoughts and convictions.

Don't get discouraged when you relapse; you didn't accumulate those negative traits in a day. It will take time and practice as well as repetition to change your thought patterns.

Your feelings and emotions, in addition to your thought corrections, play a major part, of course. Remember that without feeling, nothing comes to fruition. Even your feeling of failure is a feeling of conviction that you failed, and it is so.

"Forgiveness is not always easy. At times, it feels more painful than the wound we suffered, to forgive the one that inflicted it. And yet, there is no peace without forgiveness."
—Marianne Williamson

We have to forgive ourselves for past mistakes

By now we know that we have to forgive others. But we also have to forgive ourselves.

When you dig deep down into your subconscious and find something that brings up a bitter memory, see it for what it was, and make sure you forgive yourself, not just the "other" involved. You only acted a certain way because you didn't know better at the time. Or you knew the choice was wrong, but you had not yet begun the journey of unfoldment.

Let go of the baggage. There is no value in dragging it around. It's only a waste of space in your consciousness that could be filled with love and beauty instead of bitterness and resentment. Imagine the "hurt" leaving your Soul and good feelings coming back. Peace will be yours.

Everyone should take the time to clean out some of the accumulated stuff in their subconscious. It's time to feel and act better. You are an adult now and cannot use the excuse of immaturity anymore. You do know better now!

> **"Some choices we live not only once but a thousand times over, remembering them for the rest of our lives."**
> *—Richard Bach*

You are free to be yourself

Respect yourself and give yourself credit. You are a good thinker and reason well. You are making a sincere effort to better yourself. Your intentions are pure. You are on the road to free yourself from the limitations that held you in bondage for so long.

In your quest to be free, relax and allow the healing force of your innermost connection to the Universe, God, to infiltrate you. In this cleansing process, you can speak only to yourself; there is no "other." In your world, there is only you.

Remember, all you see around you is only the reflection of you and your world inside out. If you need guidance, go quietly within and all answers will already be available to you. Intelligence will give you what you need to know.

In your relations to others, let them "be" free also. Allow rather than interfere.

> **"I want to know all Gods thoughts;
> all the rest are just details."**
> **—*Albert Einstein***

Trust in yourself

Trust that anything you need to know will appear in your experience for a good reason. Answers will occur so you can learn and work out the problems. The challenges also show you that you still have some issues to correct. So be grateful for the daily tests. They are the road map to eternal bliss.

Fill your world with virtues of patience, courage, strength, persistence, and love.

Live your life the way you imagine, and do the things you like with the people you like. And yes, you have time to do all you want to do.

Keep criticism and judgment out of your thoughts because your future is the result of your own *now* thinking. Have no sense of fear or doubt of the future! Knowing that your "now" thought is good, you also know that your future experience will be good.

> **"I cannot imagine a God who rewards and punishes
> the objects of his creation and is but a
> reflection of human frailty."**
> **—*Albert Einstein***

"...because you can!"

Don't take on more than you should

Life is ongoing and will be yours forever. On this plane, we still have to learn that time cannot "run out." We try to cram too much into the day instead of taking time to reflect and meditate.

Don't overwhelm yourself. Take your soul off the clock. Everything you need will be accomplished. Learn how to say no. Delegate and trust that all will be done in due time. Your world is the reflection of your beliefs and convictions, and your sense of time is part of those beliefs.

> **"Music in the soul can be heard by the universe."**
> *—Lao Tzu*

What is the Ego?

According to Freud, the ego is part of the personality that mediates the demands of the ID, the super-ego, and reality. The ego prevents us from acting on our basic urges (created by the ID), but also works to achieve a balance with our moral and idealistic standards (created by the superego). While the ego operates in both the preconscious and conscious, its strong ties to the ID means that it also operates in the unconscious.

Eckhart Tolle's comment that "The extent of the ego's inability to recognize itself and see what it is doing is staggering and unbelievable" is correct. Most of the time, we act purely according to our Ego. We are not consciously choosing the right path but are unconsciously allowing the Ego to take control.

We have to leave our Ego behind.

Ego is attached to things; it loves status and always wants more material riches. It always wants something. There is always a hidden agenda behind its desires.

Ego always wants to be right, wants to be better than others, and needs an identity.

Once the Ego identifies itself with something, like a high-power job, it does not want to let go. It attaches itself to the newfound status or power. It says, "See? This is what I am."

But this is an illusion. What you are is a mental being, a soul, a powerful force of the Universe. You are more than just a job, a title, a labeled human being.

There is nothing wrong with wanting to improve your work status or aspiring to a promotion. However, the determination and aspiration should not be Ego driven; rather, it should be propelled by the motivation of higher purpose or enthusiasm or love of the work or craft.

The truth is that you are not this or that, not the corporate Alpha Male or Ms. Superwoman. The fact is that you simply are the "I AM"—nothing more, nothing less. "I AM" contains all there is.

Repeat after me: "I AM."

"...because you can!"

> **"When I admire the wonders of a sunset or the beauty of the moon, my soul expands in the worship of the creator."**
> **—Mohandas Gandhi**

Looking at the bigger picture: We are all connected, we are all one

You say you have nothing to do with the people in the Middle East or other nations at war, you disconnect yourself from the devastations of Africa, and you turn a blind eye to the homeless in your own country. I know, many of you are out there helping and volunteering, donating, and contributing necessary supplies. But you feel and see "them" as separate beings from you.

In the big picture of the Universe, when you start seeing the grand plan of the Almighty Power, there is no separation.

We are all Individuals, yet all One, like water drops in the ocean going with the current of the waves. Consciousness is one consciousness, not many. You are part of this Consciousness, like a kernel on a cob of corn. You are connected to the source. You always will be.

> **"One thing I know: the only ones among you who will be really happy are those who will have sought and found how to serve."**
> **—Albert Schweitzer**

When we think together, we become a greater force. There is mass thinking that can lead to hysteria or manipulation that can lead to panic. The results of mass thinking are very visible in the nations of war.

Mass thinking, or large group hysteria, is also responsible for the challenges with the economy. Epidemics, poverty, and economic downturns are examples of the negative effects of wrong mass thinking.

To the contrary, we see groups coming together in disaster relief efforts and many other wonderful, positive outreach programs. Positive mass thinking has an unbelievable, dynamic effect and will turn the world into a paradise—a united, loving society. Why not start now?

You are an individual and should think individually. If agreeing with a certain cause, make sure it is of high standard, noble, and worthy in the mental sense, so to speak. If you don't like what you see, don't join. Remember, however, that it's not the people that are wrong; it's their actions and their behavior.

By joining a good cause you will empower this massive force of right thought even more. With your understanding of the truth, you will be an ambassador of Light and Love.

If what you see is not good, it is not real. If what you see is good, continue to make it better. You are an important contributor to all that is good. You are goodness itself.

"Let the beauty of what you love be what you do."
—Rumi

The point of transition to the next dimension

At the point of transition to the next dimension, or so-called death, you cannot take earthly possessions with you. What you can take with you are your values, your character, your personality, the "I AM" awareness, knowledge, intelligence, and understanding—all relative to where you are in your unfoldment at the time of passing.

"There are many mansions in my father's house," as Jesus pointed out. This means that there are many dimensions or states of mind in Consciousness. We will have to pass through them as part of the ever-unfolding process.

Your earthly belongings that you leave behind will be nothing more than a dream, and they will change according to the new owner's sense of it.

For example, when someone passes, his or her house usually sits in probate. It might have been sold or given to the heirs, and the new owner's thoughts and ideas will transform it to correspond to his or her vision.

Think about it in a spiritual, mental way. It's the thought of the new owner that transforms it, his or her vision manifest. Since you are "gone," your thought and attention is withdrawn from the property. It literally "goes away" and transforms to correspond to someone else's sense.

We know that at the time of death, the Soul withdraws from the body and moves on. We leave the body behind, but the body never had life on its own and was only animated by Spirit, your Soul.

We will awaken in the next dimension to the fact that we did not die. Life cannot die; it is the opposite. Life lives. However, we will have to pick up where we left off and continue to unfold and progress toward more of Life and its perfection.

Since we can take only our understanding and character with us, the most important goal we have here on this plane is to unfold as far as possible in our understanding so that we do not have to do it all over again.

Individual consciousness will continue to solve the problems of life as it continues the journey toward perfect Intelligence. So why not gain as much understanding here and now, and eventually move on with a greater knowledge of the truth to the next plane or dimension?

> **"That which is so universal as death must be a benefit."**
> **—Friedrich Schiller**

Life is Life and cannot die

Do not jump to conclusions on this subject matter. There are many philosophies and opinions out there. No one has really experienced the hereafter and stayed on this plane long enough to be able to teach about it (except for maybe Jesus, for a brief moment).

However, it is reasonable to say that Life is Life and cannot die, or it would not be Life. You, your Soul, or Consciousness are part of this everlasting Life element and, therefore, cannot die. Death is nothing but a transition from one plane or state of mind to another, continuing the unfolding process.

You cannot stop progress. You have to abide the law.

"We are not victims of aging, sickness and death. These are part of scenery, not the seer, who is immune to any form of change. This seer is the spirit, the expression of eternal being."
—Deepak Chopra

You are the highest species on this plane

I am always looking at nature and its workings. Life is a circle and replenishes and multiplies itself constantly.

You are of the highest species in this Nature Kingdom, and your substance is perfect Intelligence. Every thing is alive: the planets, the animals, even the rocks are part of life, and all are living expressions of consciousness.

For perfect Intelligence to die would not be intelligent. Intelligence governs now and will govern the hereafter; it is and always will be.

Your real world is inside of you and not outside of you, even though the reflection appears that way. So become the leader of your world inside and out…because you can!

ANSWER THESE QUESTIONS HONESTLY:

1. What makes you happy, fulfilled, content, empowered, and strong?
2. What are you thinking most of during the day?
3. What makes you uncomfortable and why?
4. Is there a subject you'd rather not address because you think it's too painful?
5. Are you neglecting to see the good in everything? Explain why.
6. Can you forgive yourself for past mistakes?
7. Do you trust your own instincts?
8. Write down a few examples of mass thinking and its effects.
9. What is your sense of the afterlife?
10. Think about your world inside and out. Write it down. Start a journal.

CHAPTER 19

THE SPIDER EFFECT

Think of a spider web. Isn't it fascinating? It can stretch, grow bigger and bigger, and it spreads until it entangles all. One little creature can create such a magnificent structure and have such an impact.

Like the spider, we are all little creatures compared to the vastness of the Universe. But we can create a giant web of goodness because we are connected in the mental realm. We come from one source. This connection makes us powerful.

"His ambition is to be the spider in the World Wide Web."
—John McCarthy

Our ambition should be as a spider's, but in the World Wide Web—not on a website online, but in the projection of our thoughts, which can web out into the Universe, connecting us to all.

"...because you can!"

Start thinking more all-inclusive thoughts, more Universal thoughts, and more all-loving and healing thoughts. Think of a bigger picture, and don't stay in such a small vacuum (called your personal sense).

The beliefs that are held strongly in mass consciousness will be reflected in the reality of this world, good or bad. If millions of people think the same way, or expect the same outcome, it will manifest.

Again, the economy is a very good example. It reflects mass consciousness reacting to fear. You can also see this thought power in the creation of epidemics. In the extreme way, this is how wars start.

"If we have no peace, it is because we have forgotten that we belong to each other."
—*Mother Teresa*

On a positive level, as mass consciousness evolves, it shows the picture of better living, wealth, and prosperity in our world. The American people have long been known to have a prosperous attitude and a strong self sense, which has been reflected in becoming one of the world's leading nations. The collective sense of America's population has made the United States what it is today.

"If you and I are having a single thought of violence or hatred against anyone in the world at this moment, we are contributing to the wounding of the world."
—*Deepak Chopra*

We are in an age of great spiritual change

Today, people are awakening to the truth that the invisible cause and the visible effect is the result of their own right or wrong thoughts. They have come to the realization that the Universe is a mental rather than a physical, material state.

As more and more people discover this truth, the reflection (your specific life experience and environment) will change to correspond to this newfound insight.

We have to start somewhere. This somewhere is our own right thinking, which creates our own right future. From there it is only a few steps to contributing to a greater picture.

Don't underestimate collective consciousness. It is very powerful. It is a spider effect rippling out into the world. Yes, we can make a difference in this world, even though it still needs so much inspiration and healing.

> **"The learning and knowledge that we have, is, at the most, but little compared with that of which we are ignorant."**
> **—*Plato***

Metaphysical education is becoming more and more important. We have to make sure that we include our brothers and sisters on this journey with us. We must not leave anyone behind. We cannot force them to do what we want them to, but we can put the

"...because you can!"

information and our knowledge out into the Universe. They will find this treasure when they are ready and will take this journey on their own.

A good example is today's social media. Consider the twenty-four-hour media cycle during which we continuously witness how the thoughts or deeds of one person, even one in some far-off country, can impact millions of others throughout the world.

We are more closely connected to one another now than at any other time in the history of the world. So be part of this phenomenon and spread the good word; let's use the tools given to us by the inventors of technology, who are certainly being creative sources of the Universe.

> **"The most useful piece of learning for the uses of life is to unlearn what is untrue."**
> **—Antisthenes**

In this last chapter, I will reconnect all topics we have explored during this voyage together so you can see your progress. To start, we have to unlearn all that we've learned since birth. It seems like a huge task, but it is manageable. One day at a time, we will come closer to the goal of enlightenment.

We learn all the time, so embrace the new

We can choose to embrace our lives as an ongoing conscious growth process. We can make a commitment to this necessary progression. By being attentive, we can see that life is a learning experience, and I, for one, love to learn.

It is exciting to become aware of more and more that we didn't know before. We witness our mental growth and enjoy the fruits as we go through this adventure. Our awareness constantly grows and changes; it evolves and gives us a sense of comfort, security, and peace of mind.

The willingness to embrace all aspects of life, whether it's good or challenging, will further help and speed up your unfoldment. It is an ongoing series of action, never ending. You will take what you have developed and understood with you to the next dimension. Do not forget this vital point.

"As far as we can discern, the sole purpose of human existence is to kindle a light in the darkness of mere being."
—*Carl Jung*

Where do you start?

Your home is your hub. It reflects your mental house; it reflects who you are, so make it as comfortable as possible. It is important to your state of mind to be at peace in your home.

Surround yourself with pretty things, like flowers and plants, pictures and posters, and colorful ceramics; prepare a delicious meal and take the time to enjoy it. Light candles. Indulge yourself in beautiful music.

Sit outside with a hot cup of tea or a tall, cool drink. Or just read a good book in bed. Whatever gives you pleasure should be part of your daily routine.

Remember, you have to start with YOU first.

Most people have their thinking on auto-pilot. It is habitual and repetitive. You do not filter and analyze what you are thinking; instead, you are letting thoughts run wild. Thinking just happens to you and you are out of control—or at least not in the driver's seat.

It is your duty to develop a good quality of character and to continue to empty out previous concepts. It will take a great deal of willingness to refrain from taking the easy route and sliding back into your old habits. You will be climbing a mountain and not coasting along; it takes effort but you will find freedom, greater self-sufficiency, and self-confidence.

In order to really understand what is coming your way by changing your mental attitude, you must have a good heart and be strictly honest.

"It is necessary to help others, not only in our prayers, but in our daily lives. If we find we cannot help others, the least we can do is to desist from harming them."
—Dalai Lama

A better life for all

Everybody claims to want a better life and is looking for guidance to understand "how" it is achievable.

However, few make the effort to really work on the unfoldment of their Soul. In this final chapter, I will remind you of the basic points.

The individual tests you experience along the way are necessary. Put importance on your progress, always take quality before quantity, and love your correction. Do not be dependent on anyone or anything.

Look out for your own best interest first, but be fair to others. You cannot take care of anyone unless you take care of yourself first. Be compassionate and caring, but don't get involved in other people's personal affairs.

On a grander scale, don't focus on the negative, don't protest, and don't be upset about world issues, politics, or seemingly unjust occurrences. Change your sense about them, and understand that they are only a picture or reflection of mass thinking. Remember the spider effect. It all starts with you and me.

> **"Let us always meet each other with smile, for the smile is the beginning of love."**
> **—Mother Teresa**

We are actors of life

We play a role, and every day we slip into different parts of the play as actors do: Mother/father to our children, wife/ husband to our spouse, and, when we visit the doctor, we become the patient. When we go to school, attend classes, or participate in seminars, we become students. Going to work we become a mechanic, nurse, or firefighter. You might play the role of a hero, an intellectual, artist, or a victim.

We act differently in each capacity. The only thing that stays the same is our Soul, our true essence. But we are so busy playing the role that we neglect the Soul.

> **"Everything you are against weakens you.
> Everything you are for empowers you."
> —Wayne Dyer**

Your mental business is to be busy with the good. Let go of the acting part. Be who you are. You can be a mother without acting like one. You can be a husband without pretending to be the kind of husband you think you are supposed to be.

You can be an artist by expressing yourself through your art, but you don't have to play the role that you think is expected of you. Can you shed the role of victim by taking on the responsibility of victor?

What matters to you? Who are you? Are you afraid of finding out?

> **"Our thinking and our behavior are always in anticipation of a response. It is therefore fear-based."
> —Deepak Chopra**

Most people define themselves through their Ego. Our Ego is how we identify ourselves on this plane. When someone asks you who you are, you most likely state your name, followed by your vocation. You identify yourself by what you do for a living. It gives you status.

Being man-made and superficial, we need to let go of this "image" Ego. We cannot make it our focus. The Ego is not the essence of our being. It is a mirage.

This is a purely mental state with right thought as the only creative power. You can trust your own nature to show you what you really need; Ego will only show you what you think you need to impress others.

Unless you approve and respect yourself for who and what you are, the approval from anyone else is of no value. Take the personal feelings out of it. Make it impersonal. You only have to live up to your own expectations.

> **"Take praise and bitter persecution with the same equanimity of disposition."**
> *—William W. Walter*

The Spider Effect all over the world

Now that we have established our part in the spider effect, we have to use this knowledge and participate. We have to contribute to peace and harmony, which is our inherent right.

Again, you will ask, "What about the nations in war and despair?" And again, I say, all evil and horrific experiences are man-made. God, Good, The Universe did not make these conditions. Greed and ill will did.

"...because you can!"

The mass thinking or mass consciousness of certain nations caused their wars, poverty, and despair. Their lack of understanding, compassion, and love for the good of all as well as their hateful sense expresses itself in these situations. The belief in impotence and being helpless victims contributes to these incomprehensible living situations.

People have a choice in changing their sense, beliefs, and convictions. Many do not see the light and have little or no understanding of the truth. They do not know how to change their sense. We have to be the igniters; we have to light the fire within each soul on this plane.

We have to start making improvements in our own world first, starting with ourselves and rippling out to our friends and family, our associates, and so on.

Radiate your good to your family, friends, and neighbors, and soon the world will look much brighter. Don't fight against struggles and conflicts; be a contributor to peace!

"My religion is very simple. My religion is kindness."
—Dalai Lama

Look at this interesting example, reflecting what's going on right now

On my way home from a business luncheon, I saw a bus driving by with a billboard that advertised high-demand jobs. Do you know what some of the top, most wanted and available jobs are at this point in time?

Homeland security, addictions counseling, healthcare, and forensics; these are highly sought after vocations right now. Isn't it interesting that all of the listed jobs have to do with our fears?

Homeland security—because we are so afraid that terrorists are out to kill us.

Addictions counseling—because we are so out of control emotionally that we hide behind drugs and alcohol and slowly kill ourselves.

Healthcare—because we do not know how to live a healthy life and take care of ourselves. We keep smoking even though it's the number one killer; we keep drinking excessively; and many are still addicted to drugs, pacifying their emotional pain among other vices. We continue to live unhealthy lifestyles even though it will surely kill us.

Forensics—because we want to find the bad guys who killed us in the first place.

Also, think of how many other jobs are created as a result of fear. Fear of home break-ins, fear of identity theft, fear that bank or government computers will be attacked by hackers (yes, the technology field is a top-listed job), and the list goes on and on.

Isn't this interesting?

What happened to carpenters, electricians, masons, gardeners, teachers, and the service industry? What about artists, writers, musicians, painters, and all the other wonderful, loving, possible jobs? Is fear really the number one motivator today?

"Peace cannot be achieved through violence; it can only be attained through understanding."
—Ralph Waldo Emerson

Vitality and the strength to keep on going

If you want to build your spider web of goodness, start webbing the web today.

Keep the best sense you can, and build on what you know right now. Start, no matter how small.

We as Understanders have to set an example and live accordingly.

A fresh outlook on life—one without fear and full of enthusiasm, courage, and good spirit—is needed. Feed an appetite for adventure, and search for the new instead of repeating the old and safe habits, most of them deprived of inspiration. That is the right attitude in getting to work. You will need endurance and strength to get to the goal, but you can do it.

No one grows old by living a long number of years; people grow old because they give up. Retiring does not mean letting go of your ideals and hopes and aspirations.

> **"Years wrinkle the skin—but to give up enthusiasm wrinkles the Soul."**
> *—Unknown author, Eschatology*

I just love the quote above. What a wonderful comparison. Yes, youth is not a time in your life; it is a state of mind.

You are as young as your ambitions and as old as your fears. You are a bright light shining in this Universe, no matter the number on your birth certificate. You are forever young in Universal standards. Remember the Big Bang was a long, long time (in a worldly sense) ago. This is only the beginning; there is much more to come!

What we call the body, our visible ID, is the mental symbol for Intelligence, the "I" part of Universal "I"ntelligence, forever vital and young.

Entangle the world in love and happiness…

> **"Inspiration is enough to give expression to the tone in singing, especially when the song is without words."**
> *—Franz Liszt*

Spider Effect in Nature

What we call plant life, animals, oceans, nature, or people are the visible symbols of the way we are now interpreting them during our relative unfoldment.

"...because you can!"

Nature renews all creation constantly and naturally. We still see all creation as solid, but this sense will change in due time. We will realize the mentalness of all.

In reality, everything we see has a deeper meaning. Everything we experience now is our relative sense. As we progress in our unfoldment, we will recognize the true meaning and see it for what it really is. Most of all, keep it practical. There is no mystery to Life.

As the words appear on these blank sheets of papers, I am in awe. I can feel the Universe's creativity flowing through me. I have asked for the privilege of writing. I have received the answer to my prayers from this invisible source.

Yes, we are all truly connected, not just to others but to all there is on this plane. We are one with the Universe, the all mighty intelligent source of all being.

I hope I have shown you how to think in a more Universal manner. I sincerely wish to have given you guidance and to have contributed to opening your eyes. You have to do the rest...because you can!

Lastly, remember these inspiring and powerful words:

"Imagine all the people living life in peace. You may say I'm a dreamer, but I'm not the only one. I hope someday you'll join us, and the world will be as one."
—*John Lennon*

ANSWER THESE QUESTIONS HONESTLY:

1. Now that we are at the end of the chapters, your sense will have changed to a different frequency. With this newfound awareness, explain what matters to you now?
2. What are your ambitions and goals?
3. What is the right sense about aging? What is youth?
4. Are you still afraid of finding out who and what you are?
5. What part are you playing (acting out) in your life's role? Will you change?
6. Can you outline the spider web you can create?
7. How does nature relate to the spider effect?
8. How does mass consciousness work in the spider effect?
9. How can you better the world?
10. Are you ready to take the next step?

THIS IS THE BEGINNING

A new life is in front of you, ready to be enjoyed.

I sincerely hope to have given you inspiration, guidance, and a new outlook on life. It has been presented in a step-by-step manner, leading you from basic day-to-day applications to a higher sense of being.

I thank the Universe for making the words come easy to me during the writing process. I am thankful that I have learned a great deal researching and being diligent in choosing the words. Remember you can know the meaning of the words, but without the application and/or the experience, you will not gain the understanding you are looking for.

Remember to listen to the signs all around you. Hear, see, and feel...your higher thoughts will unveil themselves to you. You know what your higher thoughts are when they feel right and there is joy in them. Communication does not just consist of words. It includes intuition, feeling, and seeing the signs from nature all around you. It encompasses synchronicity and experience.

Reread the chapters as necessary. Ask the questions given at the end of each chapter often, and answer them honestly.

You have to look at effect (the visible world) in order to see cause (the invisible source of all). Cause

"...because you can!"

always comes first, so remember it is important to diagnose your woes by looking at the effects you have caused, and go back to the source for correction.

The simple illnesses featured in the Well-being chapter are the tip of the iceberg. There is a school of thought that I intentionally did not address in these writings, but will address at a later time. Those ideas specifically focus on the power of your uneasy (diseased) thoughts and the ill effects they have on your body. It will show you the corrections necessary to heal yourself. It explains in great detail the connection of your physical health to your mental health and how to prevent all ailments and diseases in the first place.

This first volume is a workbook that gives you the basic day-to-day applications and thought corrections. After reading, studying the laws, and applying what you've learned, know one thing...this is only the beginning!

If you have questions or need help, please e-mail modernthoughttheories@gmail.com

Or join our blog at www.modernthoughttheories.com

Or you can write to PO Box 931741, Hollywood, CA 90095.

Made in the USA
Charleston, SC
20 March 2012